BANJO ON MY KNEE

Music Travels In The American South

by **Oliver Gray**

Sarsen Press

Published by Sarsen Press
Copyright: Oliver Gray, 2019
Cover design and layout by Richard Williams
Photos: Birgit Gray, Paul Dominy
Cover photo by Birgit Gray

All rights reserved. No part of this book may be reproduced in any form or by any electronic or mechanical means, including information storage or retrieval systems, without permission in writing from the publisher, except by a reviewer who may quote brief passages.

Contact Oliver Gray at www.olivergray.com

ISBN: 978-1-5272-4075-9

Printed and bound by CPI Group (UK) Ltd, Croydon, CR0 4YY

Acknowledgements

Thanks for ideas and input to: Paul Dominy, Richard Williams, Andy Washington, Chris Cowan.

Thanks to the following institutions, which were invaluable for research purposes: Civil Rights Museum, Memphis; Nashville Tourist Bureau; BB King Museum, Indianola; Muscle Shoals Museum, Sheffield; Natchez Trace Visitor Centre; Stax Museum, Memphis; Loretta Lynn Museum, Hurricane Mills; Memphis Tourism Bureau; Delta Blues Museum, Clarksdale; Rock And Blues Museum, Clarksdale; Peabody Hotel, Memphis; Historic Dyess Colony, Arkansas.

This book is for Birgit Gray.

FLIGHT OF FANCY

*B*eep *beep beep beep beep beep beep beep...*
It was the sound of my plastic Casio watch that I bought twenty-five years ago from Argos. It cost me £3.50 and I've never seen the need to purchase another timepiece since. The only adjustments I've ever had to make to my Casio have been the purchase of two new plastic straps, one of which was bought in Sydney, Australia and the other in Eastleigh High Street, just a couple of weeks ago. Eastleigh still supports a small shop whose speciality is repairing timepieces and inserting batteries into watches. How it sustains itself who knows, but in five minutes, the kind Indian lady in there replaced

my strap for a mere £5, more than the watch had cost in the first place.

Nowadays, people find out what the time is by hauling their mobile phones out of their trouser pockets and checking them, which is considerably more arduous than just flicking your wrist over. I love that watch and its simplicity. The only trouble is that my eyesight is now so bad that I have to stop, drag my spectacles out of my pocket and put them on my nose before I can read the time, so actually, using a phone would probably be a less strenuous idea.

That beeping is rare for me, because I never like to be woken up before I wake up naturally, so my dear little Casio only ever gets used when I have an urgent reason to get up in the morning. One odd knock-on effect of this is that the watch will then continue to go off at six a.m. for the next few days, until I remember to switch it off. On this occasion there was a flight to be caught at 9.30 from Southampton Airport and my daughter was due to drive me down there at 7.30. It's only a ten-minute drive.

If I'm planning to fly almost anywhere, I go online

and put in Southampton as the embarkation point and see if there are any flights to where I actually want to go. If that happened to be Paris or Jersey or Guernsey or Edinburgh, it would be possible to fly straight there from Southampton, but for other destinations, as I don't mind spending time in airports at all, I'm not averse to changing planes in places like Manchester, Paris or Amsterdam. KLM is an airline that flies from Southampton to Amsterdam, from where you can catch flights to almost anywhere in the world. This is a far preferable option to getting on a bus or train to Heathrow or Gatwick and possibly having to spend a night in a hotel and then be faced with a horrible drive around the M25 late at night on return.

Southampton airport is absolutely sweet. It only has small planes and I don't mind living under its flight path because having it there is so convenient. We don't even notice the planes going over any more, unless we have visitors who are sitting in the garden and ask how we can possibly cope with it. The answer is that you can get used to almost anything. I remember when my wife Birgit's parents used to visit us from Germany.

They lived on a busy main road in Bremen and were constantly complaining that they couldn't sleep in our house because it was too quiet.

KLM is a proper airline, so if you catch one of their little planes, they give you a mini-breakfast consisting of a tiny cardboard piece of cake and a plastic cup of tea, and they don't charge you for it like a budget airline would. Before you know it, you've arrived at Schiphol airport, where the level of sophistication outdoes almost any other airport in the world. It's sparklingly clean, well-organised and the great advantage is that you are coming in to a KLM hub that links with its partner airline Delta. You only need to walk a few metres before you are checking in for your onward flight.

Just next door, there's probably the world's most expensive Starbucks but, being in holiday mood, I was happy to spend five euros on a small cup of coffee and sit down to read my copy of *Private Eye* on one of the well-used leather sofas. Unfortunately, I had failed to synch with European time and thus very nearly missed the onward connection on account of not having put my Casio forward an hour. I guess a phone would have done that automatically? Luckily not dozing, I did manage to decipher the announcement that the flight was closing and breathlessly lurched through the charmingly courteous security check and took my seat for an all-day flight to America.

This solo trip to Nashville was inspired by the fact that I had somehow made it to seventy years old but never been to the home of Country music. It seemed important to correct this omission before getting any more decrepit, so this was my birthday present to myself. The occasion was the so-called Americanafest, which is an annual celebration of "Americana" music and is built around an awards ceremony. As I intended to cover it for a music magazine, I had managed to blag myself a press pass for the entire event but for accommodation, I put myself in the hands of my friend Paul, who works for a company that has contacts with chain hotels around the US and was able to get a good deal.

Let me tell you about Paul. I met him in a godforsaken pub in the middle of Salisbury Plain in 1980. I had gone there to write a review of a local punk band and Paul was their manager. As part of the format of the magazine, you had to approach the band and ask for a list of their gear. Paul was a tiny gentleman, hiding behind the mixing desk in a room that was so full of equipment that there was hardly any space for an audience. He had peroxide dyed blonde hair, modelled on the then currently fashionable Sting, and I plucked up courage to go and speak to him. Sure enough, he was delighted to write out copious details of all the equipment in his impeccably tidy handwriting, and we exchanged phone numbers. I knew straight away on that day that we were going to be friends but never realized that it would be a lifelong friendship that would endure a divorce (his) and an emigration (also his). In the coming years, our children would become friends, we would go on holiday together as families and he and I would embark on slightly laddish cross-channel adventures, aided by the fact that he worked for P&O Ferries.

Paul now lives in Tulsa, Oklahoma with his wife and daughter, but he works extraordinarily hard in the way that only happens in America, with very small amounts of holiday and long and stressful hours. Each March, he and I indulge ourselves in a week of musical heaven at the South By Southwest Festival in Austin, Texas. Each year I try to give up this addiction, and each year I fail. For a few days, we allow ourselves to be extremely silly and behave like teenagers, even though we are actually highly responsible adults. Paul is a more responsible adult than me, in fact, because not only is he strictly vegan but he is also teetotal, neither of which I have so far managed. But his road to such virtue has been relatively rocky.

In the early years of his time in America, Paul turned into a fat bastard. This is something that he himself would not deny. He was eating unhealthily, drinking too much and discovering gradually that he was someone who couldn't have a very good relationship with alcohol. Occasionally I would find myself in the position where I would have to pretend I didn't know him, for fear that people I was talking to would associate me with his occasionally boorish behaviour. I think we all know people who can veer between extremes, and Paul is one of them. Happily, all that is way behind him and spending time with him now is a complete delight, apart, that is, from feeling physically inferior and morally lower because I do, in fact, still eat unhealthily and I also drink.

Back at Schiphol, it was time to board the plane to Minneapolis. The flights had been bought on a secondary website, so it was not clear on the ticket which seat I would be allocated. Climbing aboard a long-haul aircraft in those circumstances can be a worrying process, because you don't know what kind of seat it will be until you get to it.

One of the Sunday papers used to run a series in which celebrities were interviewed about their holiday experiences. One of the more smugly irritating comments that was made on a regular basis was, "I love being able to turn left when boarding a plane". I've never been able to turn left, because the differentiation between standard class and first class is so huge that it more than doubles the price. But nowadays it's often the case that when you turn right, you have to walk through some upper class accommodation in order to reach the plebs' bit.

Certain things strike you immediately. Firstly, you can't really tell whether people are rich just by looking at them. All the people sitting in the posh bit, already sipping their plastic glasses of champagne, look pretty much normal, yet the truth must be that either they are extremely wealthy or they are important and successful enough for their companies to be paying for their seats.

As we troop by towards the lower class land beyond the curtain, I'm not quite sure that I would actually want to be where the poshos are. Cheap champagne doesn't appeal to me, especially in the morning, and the little pod things that they sit / lie in look just as uncomfortable as the seats we are going to have to occupy. Above all, they are not separated from all the people around them, who are just as likely to snore and fart as we are. What would be nice (and possibly worth the mark-up) would be a completely separate, sealed compartment, but as it is, it can't possibly be worth all that extra money. Actually, what they are paying for is to be kept separate from the riff-raff. It's exactly the same on a train, where people pay a huge premium to sit in a seat that is a different colour from the norm, but probably have fewer other passengers around them.

Most long-haul aeroplanes are configured in the most inconvenient way possible, that is, three rows of three seats. People travelling in groups of three are rare, so as a solo traveller, you are likely to end up either in between two other strangers, inside a couple or outside a couple. Any of these options will entail either you climbing over them or them climbing over you whenever the call of nature occurs. But right at the back of the plane, just by the loo, there is one row with just two seats and by some miracle, I had been placed in one of those. This part of the plane has a couple of advantages: it's very near the toilet and it's very near the kitchen, but these are outweighed by the disadvantages: you will be the last to receive your food (they roll the trolley all the way to the front first) and you will be shuddering from the explosive sound of the violent flushing mechanism of the toilet behind you, which is in use pretty much the entire flight.

The inside seat is the less attractive one for claustrophobia sufferers, especially if the person who turns up to sit next to you has any kind of obesity problem. At my age, there is an incipient prostate issue going on, which means enormous amounts of leg crossing in order to avoid having to ask your companion to stand up and let you through every couple of hours.

If, however, you are lucky enough to be in the outside seat, you will be the one who has to stand up whenever your companion feels the call of nature.

There are various other things to look out for, and fear number one is being next to someone with a severe cold, who is likely to cough and sneeze for the entire journey, and doubtless infect you in due course. This is one of the many unique things about being in an aeroplane. There are few other situations where you are, by necessity, so close and almost intimate with someone you have never met and would probably never have wished to meet. The next fear is that your neighbour will be wanting to make conversation. I am a perfectly sociable person but I don't want to spend hours talking to someone I may well have nothing in common with. On the contrary, I look forward to flights as an opportunity to switch off and relax.

Not many people think of aeroplanes as a relaxing environment, but they suit me down to the ground. It's hard to explain, because I have almost every phobia and irrational fear known to mankind, but for some reason I love flying. I think it's the knowledge that someone else is in charge of your destiny and you can't possibly do anything about it. It's one of the few times in life that I actually feel superior to certain others, as I observe them fidgeting and twitching. You can spot straight away who has a fear of flying and who doesn't. Thus, you can immerse yourself in distractions such as reading or doing crosswords and, above all, you can sleep.

So, sleeping on planes: Many people find this a challenge, but not me. I'm well schooled in yoga and relaxation techniques and spend most of any flight in slumberland. That, however, in itself can induce some potential issues. I don't think I snore but it's possible that I do. Certainly, I have experienced many loud snorers next to me that not even the free earplugs can shut out. So, to be safe, I normally apologize in advance to my neighbour in case snoring might occur. Farting is a more sensitive issue. I know damn well I fart in my sleep but also I know, at least I think I know, that I can control it even while asleep. I am not 100 percent sure of this, though, so as a precautionary measure I wrap myself up in my airline-provided blanket, carefully tucking it in all round me. With any luck, that ought to keep the fumes captive.

On this occasion, I found myself in the outer seat, the ideal position for a little bit more legroom. Leg stretching is very important for comfort while asleep but I have been known to send enthusiastic flight crew sprawling to the floor as they thunder down the narrow aisle on some unspecified mission. I have also received severe bruising from being smashed into by the food trolley.

If you travel on Delta, you will find yourself being offered food and drink more or less constantly. It seems to fulfil every cliché about American dietary habits. First of all, pretty much as soon as you've reached cruising height, they will come along with a little dinky bag of nuts or mini-bagels and any kind of drink you might want. On this occasion, the stewardess took one look at me and plonked two cans of beer onto the plastic tray, declaring, "You look thirsty". It was true, I was thirsty, and alcohol can help contribute to getting to sleep. On the other hand, it also contributes to a full bladder, but for that circumstance I was in the perfect seat.

Before you're halfway through your drink, the first meal arrives, accompanied by wine. My friend the stewardess immediately gave me two small plastic bottles of white wine. I must have looked as if I needed it. To be honest, I don't normally drink wine, in fact I don't even particularly like it, but I'm certainly not going to turn down anything that is free.

I'm not entirely vegetarian, it's just that I'm not that keen on meat, but ordering a vegetarian meal on an airline hasn't been a good experience. They tend to consist of a bit of salad and some bread. However, there will always be something along the lines of vegetable lasagne or vegetable curry on the normal menu. This is where being in the last seat can be a disadvantage, because often there will be no choice by the time the trolley reaches you. On Delta, they still give you a physical menu, which turns out to be largely a waste of paper, as nobody looks at it and everyone asks the stewardess what is available.

So there is your meal in front of you, and once again, the proximity to your neighbour presents challenges, on account of the extreme narrowness of the seat. To eat normally, you have to stick your elbows out, nudging your companion on one side and risking being smacked into by the trolley on the other. The amount of plastic and waste on your tray is just astonishing. Every single item is encased in plastic: there's a tiny salad with a sachet of salad dressing; there's a rock hard semi-frozen bread roll encased in cellophane; in slightly more substantial cellophane is a rubbery piece of cheese which is very difficult to extract and insert between the two water biscuits, which are also wrapped in cellophane. The wine bottle is plastic, the water bottle is plastic, the orange juice is in a plastic carton and there is a plastic glass to pour the drinks into. The main course is in a plastic container and is invariably swimming in grease and particularly hard to attack with the inevitably very flimsy plastic knife and fork. Finally, there is some kind of chocolate pudding, also in a plastic container.

Trying to manipulate any of these items risks spilling or splattering onto your neighbour. Most challenging is what to do with all the packaging as you have emptied it. For some reason, it seems to add up to far more than was originally on the tray, spilling over onto the floor or onto your trousers or onto your neighbour's trousers. Somehow it all has to be squashed back into the tray and the lid replaced, ready for it to be handed back to the stewardess.

As the staff hand out the meals to all the people around you, you are painfully aware that your head is exactly at their crotch level. It's hard to think of any other situation that offers this challenging experience. It's caused by the seats being so low and the aisle being so narrow and the fact that the staff member has to stand so close to you for such a long time. Where else are you so close to a stranger's private parts? A hairdresser is behind you, a waiter or waitress is less close to you and if you're standing on a tube train, it's the armpit rather than the groin that you're adjacent to. So while they're there, you have to decide where to look. It would be rude to look at your neighbour, so you have to keep your eyes fixed straight ahead on the little screen, or your head buried in a book.

Regarding in-flight entertainment, I rarely switch the screen on, because I find this a totally unsuitable environment for watching a film. Those cheap horrible earphones make the listening experience unbearable and I certainly don't want to carry around those huge BBC style headsets that are currently so fashionable.

The screens are extremely low definition, whereas the whole essence of a film is supposed to be as a "big screen experience", not something to watch at A5 size. Even so, as the cabin crew member is standing next to me, I invariably pretend to be engrossed in whatever is on the screen, usually that flight path monitor in which a tiny plane never seems to move.

Post-chocolate pudding, I'm normally gasping for a cuppa, but by the time the teapot reaches you, the tea is invariably stewed and bitter. I've tried asking for decaf coffee but that normally causes all sorts of controversy.

"Sharon, have you got any decaf?"

"No, sorry, have you, Clive?"

"No, sorry, have you, Dennis?"

"Sorry sir, I'm afraid we don't have any decaf."

Stewed tea it is, then, and after that comes the wait for the tray to be collected again. You daren't move an inch because the lid hasn't been able to be properly replaced and the slightest twitch could hurl all the refuse either onto the floor or onto your companion. Meantime, the effect of two cans of lager, two bottles of white wine and a cup of stewed tea mean that it is essential for you to stand up and consign your bladder contents into the minuscule facilities. My goodness, those toilets are tiny. Looking at the size and shape of some of the passengers, it's a miracle that some of them ever are able to emerge, as surely their stomachs will have touched both sides.

I'll happily admit that, like most people, I love the idea of joining the mile-high club. However, I just don't see how it's feasible. First off, there just isn't room and secondly, there's always a queue anyway. It would be hard to concentrate with somebody hammering on the door. Maybe those who "turn left" have more suitable facilities. I'll never know.

Before you emerge, you have to press the flushing mechanism. That thing really is frightening. There's a sound like a clap of thunder and an effect like a giant sea monster taking a huge intake of breath, as the contents of the bowl are sucked away with the force of a small earthquake. Why do aeroplane toilets behave completely differently from any other toilets? I'm sure there's a technical reason but I'm not sure what it is.

Delta is an airline that provides you with plenty of extras, and one of the most useful is the blackout eye patches. Soon, hopefully, the lights will dim and you will be able to commence your slumber, but first there are various other matters to be dealt with. Invariably, the person in the seat of front of you will turn out to be morbidly obese and will hurl him or herself down onto it, causing the whole row to shake violently, before reclining their seat so that you almost get a broken nose as it hurtles towards you. If you're in a normal seat, you then have to face the unpleasantness caused by you, in turn, reclining your seat and annoying the person behind you. This causes a domino effect, where you have to blame the passenger in front of you, that person blames the person in front of them etc, etc. But in the seat I happened to be in on this flight to Minneapolis, I had no choice. The back seat didn't recline at all, so it was a matter of accepting I was going to be spending the next eight hours like a sardine in a tin. There was nothing else for it but to don the eye patches, insert the earplugs, commence the breathing exercises, put the self-hypnosis into action and pray the person next door had a stronger bladder than me.

As it turned out, I can't remember anything about my

neighbour at all, so he or she must have been free of any viruses or afflictions. The next thing I was aware of was a slightly fowsty aroma, making it clear that the pre-arrival snack had been placed on my tray. I'd missed several more rounds of drinks and an ice-lolly, apparently. The arrival of the snack is another unsatisfactory aspect of flying. So that everything can be cleared away in time for landing, it is delivered ninety minutes ahead of arrival. Having done nothing but sleep since the last enormous meal, I had really no need to have it at all, but as it was a tempting slice of pizza, I took a few desultory bites. Then, for an hour, there was little to do except stare desperately at the still semi-stationary little plane on the screen. All around, the other passengers slept peacefully through the delivery and eventual untouched collection of the snack.

Arrival in Minneapolis caused me a certain amount of stress, because I was at the very back of the plane and needed to be at the very front of the queue in order to facilitate the connection. For this, I had the potentially adequate time of one hour and forty minutes. Of course, it's impossible to push to the front in this circumstance.

You are told to remain with your seatbelt fastened until the light goes out. Being an obedient sort of person, I obeyed the instruction, but of course everybody around me immediately started unclicking themselves and standing up. They instantly opened the overhead lockers and started pulling out their possessions. By the time I stood up, the aisle was already completely full of passengers, all of whom were now ahead of me in the queue.

There was no need to be nervous yet. If all went well, the time ought to be ample, but of course, all did not go well. The initial impression was positive, because there was an automated passport checking system that actually worked. I felt quite confident that there might even be time for a snack before grabbing the next plane. Unfortunately, the automated system was immediately followed by a traditional non-automated system, which involved the customary mile long queue (or "line", as they call it) snaking to and fro along the corridors created by little poles and ropes. It's one of life's more humiliating experiences, as you shuffle along, trying not to make eye contact with anyone. I was desperate not to reveal how my heart rate was going up and my sweat glands becoming agitated as I consulted my trusty Casio.

What could those immigration officials have been asking the passengers? Whatever it was seemed to be taking an inordinately long time per person, but eventually I reached the front of the queue and was allotted another mini-queue for the next available booth. Unbelievably, and extremely nerve-rackingly, it turned out that the completely innocuous-looking lady in front of me must have had something wrong with her documentation, because she took over twenty-five minutes to process. In fact she wasn't processed, because eventually a couple of heavies came along and escorted her off to an interrogation room.

Then there was the usual rigmarole of collecting your luggage and re-checking it in. "There's no way in a million years that'll get to Nashville with me," I thought. I had a bad ankle and the last thing I wanted to do was run anywhere, but as the onward flight was due in a matter of minutes, run I had to, eventually puffing up to the desk just as the flight was about to close. Americans, of course, take all this stuff in their stride, treating the whole process like we would if catching a bus, and probably are quite happy just to get the next plane, but I was in a state of panic about what might or might not happen to my checked luggage.

The flight to Nashville took a mere thirty minutes and it was easy to find the place where Paul would pick me up, right in front of the airport. As usual, my phone refused to work but he came anyway, having tracked the flight arrival. He, of course, has a huge people carrier, and every vehicle cruising round was a huge people carrier, so identifying him wasn't easy.

It turned out the hotel was only five minutes from the airport and, before I knew it, I was having that unique American chain hotel experience which entails marvelling at a bed the size of a small tennis court, turning off the vicious air conditioning and confirming that there were no tea and coffee making facilities such as you might find in a UK establishment. Actually, this being a three-star hotel, there was indeed a coffee machine but, as I hardly ever drink coffee, this wasn't much use. I had brought my decaf tea bags with me, but any attempt to create hot water for tea failed and the resulting brew tasted like cold coffee on account of the water running through the machine. But help was at hand: Dear Paul had come up with the perfect birthday present for me and delivered it in the nick of time. Yes, an electric kettle and a hairdryer, both with American plugs. No gift could have given me greater pleasure, and I know they will give me endless service for many years to come.

One thing that Paul does for me when we go on our musical trips is briefly suspend his teetotalism, so that we can enjoy the odd beer together. This is impressive, I think, because it demonstrates a confidence in his lack of dependency on alcohol. For a few short days, he will join me in a couple of beers, but won't drink alcohol for the next 12 months, and won't miss it. In the bad old days in Austin, Paul's weak bladder could cause all sorts of problems. After drinking numerous alcoholic beverages, he would suddenly need to pee, but of course there are hardly any public toilets in American cities. Therefore he would need to dive into some bar or restaurant in order to carry out the necessary bladder emptying, which was invariably extremely urgent. My suggestion that he should just go behind a bush or down an alleyway would cause Paul to deliver a stern lecture on the dangers of such a course of action on America. According to Paul, he would likely be immediately detained as a potential sex offender. On the rare occasion when I would ignore his advice, he would plead with me almost on bended knee not to do it, saying that I was bound to be arrested.

More often than not, a particular venue for toilet activity turned out to be the Radisson hotel in central Austin, where the facilities are suitably plush. Paul would disappear through the revolving door, trying to look as though he was a hotel guest. Personally, I found this more cringeworthy then taking the risk of being arrested, but anyway, it is no longer relevant because Paul has changed his ways. To celebrate this, in 2016, we went as far as to spend over an hour in a copy shop creating and laminating a plaque saying "The PJ Dominy Memorial Restroom", which we duly affixed to the door of the bathroom with Blu-Tak. What the guests thought of it will remain unknown.

So the first destination in Nashville was the gas station over the road for some delightfully cheap cans of Modelo beer, to be stored for later. But already, I was being demanding. The moment I land in America, I require Mexican food. Immediately. So I requested that we should drive straight into town and search for a Mexican restaurant. That meant we got off to a bad start, because there was the launch of a new venue happening on Broadway, the central Nashville music strip. It was like some festival, with the street closed to traffic, huge screens, deafening music, ridiculous overcrowding and drunk people staggering around. The search for a Mexican restaurant was quite a challenge, desperately following Paul's Google Maps, which led us to two closed restaurants and finally one open one, Bakersfield, which turned out to serve lovely (expensive) food and even more lovely (cheap) beer.

Feeling better, we returned to find that we'd been duped into using a church-owned car park and had, of course, misunderstood the conditions, meaning there was an eighty-dollar fine attached to the windscreen. If there is a God, we're destined for Hell because of what we said about Christians and their car parks that night.

NASHVILLE SKYLINE

In the morning, Paul was complaining about being woken by the smell of bacon, which, to a vegan, isn't a good start to the day. Breakfast finished serving at 9 a.m., so I was there at 8.59, but not before a rude awakening at 6 a.m.

Beep beep beep beep beep beep beep beep ...

Bugger, bugger, bugger, why hadn't I remembered to switch off the Casio? Now I found myself hurling my way round the room in the dark, trying to locate my elusive little plastic friend. Then I managed to press all the wrong buttons, thus activating several of its other features, such as the stopwatch, which I didn't switch off until three days later, when I realised it was still going.

The small dining room was already full of large, sweaty people whose plates were piled up high. Some of them had bacon, egg, muffins (the sweet ones) fruit and cereals all on the same plate but, unlike Paul, I was pleased and surprised to see the bacon and the eggs, because not all American hotels make such delicacies available. Whether or not you could describe them as delicacies was debatable, because the scrambled eggs had clearly been made with egg powder and the bacon was so hard that you could have picked up two rashers and used them as drumsticks. The debris left at the end of one of these meals is arguably even worse than that left on your airline tray, because every item has copious packaging and nothing is reusable. Therefore, there was one employee whose sole job was to empty the dustbin every few minutes.

Today's first job was to pick up our credentials. When I had applied for a press pass, I put Paul down as my official photographer. For many years, at other festivals, this has been a downright lie, because he was not a photographer at all. However, in recent years he has blossomed into a superb photographer and therefore his bona fides are completely legitimate.

The headquarters of the AMA organisation had been set up in a hotel called the Westin, which we now had to find somehow. Having agreed that Paul would not be driving, on account of his willingness to indulge in the occasional beer, I was determined to prove everyone wrong on the matter of public transport. You will always be told that American public transport is non-existent, but already I had worked out from a comment on the hotel's Trip Advisor page that there was a bus stop just outside. The lady on reception had no idea where it would be but I could actually see it from the front window. You had to walk across a large car park and negotiate an eight-lane highway to get to it, but it was definitely there. I could see the sun reflecting off its plastic windows.

Waiting at this stop was always interesting, because you never had any idea when the bus was likely to turn up and there was always a motley collection of fellow passengers waiting at the stop among the piles of uncollected litter. As this was just on the edge of the forecourt of a Shell garage, I was at a loss to understand why nobody showed any sign of clearing the mess up. If I'd stayed much longer, I'd have gone out there with a black bin liner and picked it up myself, even though I could spot the odd used needle among it.

I was glad that I had brought along a peaked cap, because the temperature was already well over 100 degrees and the bus stop offered no shade. Paul remembered he had left something vital back in the hotel and so disappeared to collect it. Of course, a bus came along in the meantime and I had to ignore it.

Buses in the UK, outside of London, tend to be used only by schoolchildren and the very elderly, on account of the free bus passes which, at the time of writing, are available to pensioners. In the US, however, buses are the domain of the poor. None of my American friends take buses anywhere and one regular feature of the week in Nashville was their complete disbelief and astonishment when I told them we were travelling around by bus. Yet this particular bus took us all the way from the outskirts, right into the centre of the city, dropping us off at Broadway. The price - get this - was $1.20 return. That seems to me to be a very fair transport system and it also explains how it was that many of the passengers were clearly extremely deprived, both in their demeanour and their clothing. In a way that can be observed in other parts of the American South, there is also a clear racial divide, with 80 percent of the passengers being black. It's quite a sociable experience, with both drivers and passengers being chatty and friendly.

Once in town, we had to find where the Westin was. Stealing a map from a tour bus office, we identified its location and started to walk. Nashville turned out to be actually quite hilly and we could see the tower block from a distance, but it never seemed to get any nearer. Eventual arrival took us into a queue for our passes, but this ended in disappointment, because it turned out that Paul was only entitled to a wristband, rather than a photo pass. That this was a disadvantage was immediately clear, because I wanted to attend a workshop about a record company, which was taking place in the same building. Despite the fact that it was only a quarter full, Paul wasn't allowed in, but in the end it wasn't interesting enough for me to want to stay anyway. Would this cause problems during the rest of the week? We would see.

This being the eve of the actual festival, there wasn't much going on, but I had set my sights on a showcase organised by the BMI, which is some kind of American music industry body, I think the one that collects publishing royalties. On the way there, we spent a considerable time searching for something to eat and, having entered and then left several establishments, ended up making the error of choosing a hipster place which was extremely expensive and crap. At the time, we didn't know that there was going to be free food at the showcase. Eventually, locating the BMI building, we realised that there must be still some money sloshing around in the music industry, as it was a brand new and extremely sumptuous edifice, packed with very expensive equipment. The concert was taking place on the roof garden, which had panoramic views over the city in all directions. The stage was set up in such a way that the artists seemed to be playing in the sky. In a way it was quite exciting, but it was also intimidating, because we were surrounded by music business people and basically we were a fraud. In those circumstances, you are best advised to avoid eye contact in case anyone asks you who you are and what you do.

The lineup was quite appealing. First, there was an interesting duo who turned out to be one of the hits of the festival. They were called, oddly, The War And Treaty and certainly were by no means "Americana". Soul-pop would be a more accurate description, but of course they had added a be-stetsoned pedal steel player to lend authenticity. I went off them when they started dedicating songs to "our brave troops".

Then came something that I was half dreading and half looking forward to. Many years ago I'd put on a concert by someone called Israel Nash Gripka, who, very unusually for an American musician, behaved in a really obnoxious manner. I swore never to go and see him again and certainly never to host him again. However, he was on this bill and I had decided to let bygones be bygones and give him another go. In fact, it was quite appealing because, in the meantime, he had shortened his name to Israel Nash and built up a reputation of being a fantastic live performer. I was fully anticipating having to do a volte-face and being able to take pleasure in eating my words. I just prayed he wouldn't recognise me, but then why would he?

As it turned out, it was a pretty standard country rock show, which was bearable but nothing special, by contrast to the main act for the evening, who was the legendary swamp rocker Tony Joe White. He could hardly have been more out of place among the inattentive hipsters, some of whom had no idea who he was but were pleasantly surprised when he performed some of the songs he had written for other artists, such as "Rainy Night In Georgia". He and his band established a funky groove which didn't last nearly long enough. As I sipped my free but absolutely disgusting artisan beer, it did cross my mind that he didn't look too well. Nonetheless, it was a shock to read, just a month later, that he had passed away.

Neither Paul nor I had any knowledge of the geography of Nashville. I could have done some advance research, but basically I had just never got round to it. Nashville is renowned for its honky-tonk bars but also famous for gentrification, meaning that the genuine music bars are rapidly disappearing. We'd been told that the most authentic one was held in a social club in East Nashville called American Legion. As luck would have it, this is a weekly event held on Tuesdays and it was indeed a Tuesday, but how to get there? We hadn't realised that there were two Nashvilles, one on each side of the river. We were in West Nashville and we needed to be in East Nashville, by all accounts the cool area where the best and most authentic music can be found. There was nothing for it but to take an Uber, something that in my mind is akin to a taxi, and taxis are anathema to me on account of being expensive. Thus began an accumulation of Uber bills that built up on Paul's credit card and eventually added up to rather too much money by the end of the week.

Moods are strange things, and mine can be affected by climate and jet lag. Even as we arrived in the packed car park of American Legion, I was starting to feel a bit strange and uncomfortable, and this didn't improve as we entered a very peculiar environment. The building had several rooms and was quite seriously overcrowded. It seemed to be a place where people went to see and be seen, rather like they used to do in London in the days of the New Romantics. People were dressed up to the nines in Country music gear, some of it clearly quite expensive and exclusive. Flamboyant shirts and enormous hats, flowing beards and hideous belt buckles abounded.

The very first thing that happened was that I hesitated on entering the main room and was immediately berated from behind by somebody who claimed that I was blocking his view. As he was sitting on a chair towards the back of a very overcrowded room full of standing people, this seemed an unfair accusation, but I didn't have anywhere else to move to, and so retreated to the bar to try and find a drink, even though the queue was ten deep.

I felt even more out of place when being introduced to a young English musician called Josh O'Keefe, who had moved to Nashville in his teens in order to make his fortune. For some reason, Paul knew him from a festival he'd attended in Oklahoma. Josh is a nice guy with a rather charming Woody Guthrie fixation, but my brain wasn't functioning enough to engage in conversation with his father, who'd arrived from Derby to visit his son and was determined to chat, even though it was impossible to hear a word he was saying. This is something else that causes me difficulty - trying to converse in a loud environment. I'm certainly not deaf but the jumble of noises made it confusing. Once again, I attempted a retreat in order to find a quiet spot, which was a hopeless mission.

Just then, I spotted someone I recognized. It was Robyn Hitchcock, a British musician who comes originally from the part of the UK where I live, but who has long since relocated to Nashville. In America, he is revered as an Olde Englishe treasure, and I could see people nudging each other and pointing at him. He's certainly not easy to overlook, as he is six feet four tall and specialises in tasteful but garish psychedelic shirts. Over the years, I had had numerous encounters with Robyn and never before had he recognised or acknowledged me, but in this case he not only saw me but even remembered my name. Although rather thrilling, this was not as good as it might have seemed, because I immediately became very nervous and starstruck. I managed to stumble through a brief conversation before he introduced me to a British guitarist called John Smith. This guy is a very fine musician and really I should have been buttering him up in the hope of getting him to do a gig for us, but in my nervousness, all I could think of saying was that John Smith must be a terrible name for an aspiring artist who would hope that people would search for him on the internet. I don't think he was impressed by the comment but I couldn't tell because I couldn't understand anything he said.

In the end, I found a spot squashed into a corner and listened to some of the music. There was a tremendous amount of back-slapping going on, with much expressing of what an "honor" it was to share the stage with so-and-so. Despite the fame of some of the performers, such as Robbie Fulks and Jim Lauderdale, I disliked all of it. My relationship with Country music is ambivalent at best, but basically, I was just in a bad mood and feared that it would bode ill for the rest of the week. As the Uber took forever to get back to the hotel and the dollar signs in my head began to reach panic level, I began to wonder if this trip had been a bad mistake.

Breakfast again finished at nine but was already paid

for, so, being on a budget, I devised a simple solution, entailing getting up, eating, and then going back to bed for three hours. This meant that I was refreshed and ready to face the day round about lunchtime. Today was the day of the Americana Awards and my trusty pass gave me admission to the ceremony, which was to be held at the famous Ryman Auditorium. Originally constructed in 1892 as the Union Gospel Auditorium, the Ryman had rapidly become an important centre for Country music. The Grand Ole Opry TV show was broadcast there for over thirty years, having allegedly moved there from previous venues because the Ryman's wooden seats were vandal-proof. It was rescued from demolition after falling into decay in the mid-twentieth century, restored to a full-scale concert hall in the 1990s and renovated yet again in 2015. Its Country music history made it a fitting place for the Americana Awards to be held.

But what is Americana? Now that's a can of worms that needs an entire book of its own. Indeed, there have already been numerous books on the subject, beginning with Professor Brian Hinton's "South By Southwest: A Roadmap To Alternative Country". I have witnessed some quite stormy arguments on social media about what Americana actually is, and when it comes to identifying "UK Americana" (of which a substantial delegation was present in Nashville), well, I just lose the will to live. But, as I am allegedly an Americana promoter, I have felt obliged to attempt my own definition. I am actually quite pleased with it, because it sums up my own feelings, and it is a genre that can really only be defined as each person understands it. Therefore, discussions as to whether so-and-so can be described as Americana are doomed to end in stalemate. Unless, of course, you think an Eton-educated shouty British punk singer is Americana. There I draw the line.

Here's what I wrote when attempting a definition of Alt-Country and Americana:

"Nobody knows who invented the expression "Alternative Country" - some frazzled publicist, no doubt - but actually, for me, it's Country sensibility mixed with a rock, and even punk, attitude. Checked shirts, twangy guitars, riffs, loping, swinging basslines and lyrics that can go anywhere. A peculiar yearning pathos that's hard to explain. What about Americana then? I am simply struggling to tell you what music I like and basically, it

is anything that is American and alternative, all the way from Jackson Browne to the New York Dolls. That'll have to do you. Writers have devoted several hundred pages of prose to explaining this music but I can do it in two words: Kathleen Edwards. If you love her music, you're a friend of mine."

Still wondering? Go out and buy yourself a Kathleen Edwards album then. She's Canadian, by the way.

The trek to the Ryman was to be a solo outing, because Paul didn't have a photo pass. Not that this would have made any difference, because photography was strictly forbidden in the venue anyway. I braved the highway and arrived at the bus stop in time to witness a blazing argument between two young people who appeared to be under the influence of drugs. As they both had wild looks in their eyes, I made sure to look the other way and whistle to myself.

The payment system for the bus was remarkably simple: You simply stuffed a couple of dollar bills into a machine next to the driver and your ticket popped out. Any money left over was retained on the ticket for future journeys, something I didn't understand sufficiently at the time.

For those who say public transport is useless in

America, I can respond that the bus was air-conditioned, fast and clean. In front of me and behind me were two ladies, both of whom were having very loud phone conversations with members of their families. It was hard to keep track of which crisis was which and I felt a bit nosey, even though I had no choice but to listen in. I transferred my attention to the guy on the other side of the bus. He, too, was on the phone and had a handful of coins and bills. He was describing them in great detail to whoever was on the other end of the phone, seemingly a dealer in money, who was adjudicating as to whether his coins and bills had any rarity value. This seemed to be quite a good hobby for someone who clearly was down on his luck.

The road into town was long and straight and there was plenty to see from the windows, including numerous malls, an automobile museum and, at one stage, a whole row of gun and ammunition shops. It probably would never have entered my head to worry about the fact that people around me might be toting firearms, had it not been for an incident in the Broken Spoke venue in Austin two years before. I was queuing for the bar and, as I turned around, the rucksack I had on my back lightly brushed the woman in front of me. She whirled around and accused me of touching her inappropriately. My response was, of course, horror and copious apologies for not paying more attention. My English accent is normally deemed to be endearing to my American friends, and indeed has been an instigator for many pleasant and friendly conversations from people overhearing me and interjecting that international form of introduction, "Where you from?" This didn't apply to this lady, who accused me of being a limey asshole and informed me that her husband would be arriving shortly and had a gun. That was quite enough for me and within seconds I was outside the venue, trying to hail a taxi.

The nearest stop to Broadway was outside a bar called the Crab Shack, next to a rather tacky-looking Johnny Cash museum. Hardly had I descended, when I realised that I had failed to put my press lanyard around my neck on leaving the hotel, which meant that I wouldn't be able to get into the awards ceremony. Never mind, there was plenty of time, so all I needed to do was go back by bus and pick it up. But there was a problem. Anyone who has travelled by bus in any cities that have one-way streets will know that it's not straightforward to locate the bus stop for returning to where one came from. It won't simply be on the other side of the street, because the traffic only flows in one direction. I tried asking people in souvenir shops and tourist bus booths and nobody knew. In the end, I had to walk a considerable distance to the tourist information office, and even there, the staff had to have a lengthy discussion and look it up on the internet before establishing where the bus stop was.

It was half an hour to the hotel and half an hour back again, and, despite not having made any progress, I did at least have my lanyard. I was thinking I'd have to use it to get into a nearby bar where a showcase was taking place for a UK distribution company, but in fact nobody took any notice and there was hardly anyone there anyway. I did note with some dismay that much of the audience ignored the performers and talked most of the way through. In an adjacent room, I bumped into an English songwriter called Robert Vincent and he bought me a beer, causing me some embarrassment because I had to rush off quite soon afterwards and couldn't repay him. I know the conditions of near penury that most singer-songwriters live in and I resolved to make it good as soon as I could.

It was time to head towards the Ryman Auditorium, which entailed a trek along Broadway, this time with slightly smaller crowds. Each bar contained a not very good band. I had already gathered that these groups are largely peopled by youngsters, in Nashville to try and seek their fortune. This is a way for them to make enough money to survive. It means that they have to do endless requests for the many tourists who throng the city centre, and work for tips, which people throw in a bucket. Essentially, they are almost busking, mentioning pointedly between each song how important it is that we should contribute to the tip jar. Musicians I spoke to were quite clear that it was compulsory only to play covers. This was not the Nashville I had had in mind at all, but maybe things would be different at the awards ceremony.

I puffed up the hill and into a queue to get into the Ryman. It is indeed an impressive building, still having a churchy feel. All the pews are made of wood, which did explain why every artist immediately received a lengthy standing ovation, inspired less by the performance and more by the need to address the problem of a numb bum. I was surrounded by large numbers of mainly European music journalists and agents, presumably on expense accounts because they were indulging in copious amounts of beer at nine dollars a plastic glass. Or maybe they were Norwegian and thought they were getting a bargain? Behaviour was monitored by a SWAT team of very strict old ladies with torches and signs saying "No Photography", which were completely ignored by the Dutch journalist next to me, who shielded his iPhone with his hand as he illegally filmed the entire event.

Having never attended an awards ceremony before, I fully expected it to consist of people telling each other how wonderful they were, and indeed that is exactly what happened. There was a well-drilled house band which backed all the nominees as they came on and did their turns, consisting of a single song each, which was deeply unsatisfying.

There were, however, some excellent highspots. These included Rosanne Cash making a lengthy political speech which had some of the more Country orientated members of the audience squirming, a lifetime achievement award for a rather ill-looking John Prine, and a superbly rebellious slot by Tyler Childers, who greeted his Emerging Artist Of The Year award by being clearly contemptuous of the entire affair. He horrified the organisers by announcing, "Americana ain't no part of nothin' … It kinda feels like purgatory". Then, to great hilarity, he pointed out that his name should be pronounced Chillders rather than Chylders, which every presenter had got wrong all evening, only for the next announcer to pronounce it the same way as everybody else had.

It was worth being there alone for an incredible tour de force performance of "Let Your Kindness Remain" by Courtney Marie Andrews, and to have that warm feeling of seeing an artist who is clearly going to be a gigantic star. The event was ultimately unsatisfying, but did have some very funny moments, such as a song by Canadian compères the Milk Carton Kids, which was delightfully disrespectful in its attempt to define Americana. Oh, and despite the entire event clearly having been rehearsed down to the millisecond, there was still a major sound breakdown, which caused a fifteen-minute delay while technicians rushed around frantically.

By the end, I was starving and desperate for a beer (I ain't paying nine dollars for a beer under any circumstances). Paul was waiting outside and, for want of any better option, we went straight back to the Bakersfield Mexican restaurant where we had been the night before and ordered exactly the same as we had had then. This we walked off with a marathon hike to one of the main Americanafest venues, a truly horrible place called the Cannery, which consists of three venues that overlap into each other, causing awful sound leakage. It was also the only official venue we encountered that featured unfriendly security staff and frighteningly severe overcrowding. I had had high hopes for the evening, which was a Creedence Clearwater Revival session featuring many of the artists in town for the festival, but in the end it was impossible either to see or hear. There was no point in hanging around, plus I was astonished and infuriated to hear that they were playing the Ike and Tina Turner version of Proud Mary, rather than Creedence's original. This was sacrilege and gave us a good excuse for an early night.

The following morning saw a repeat of the breakfast ritual. To be frank, it was only day three and I was already getting sick of scrambled eggs and cardboard bacon, but it was free and therefore had to be eaten. I have something approaching a phobia about eating early in the morning. I normally wake up not feeling remotely hungry, especially if I've eaten late the night before and done nothing other than sleep in the interim; no energy has been expended and therefore no nutrition is required. That's what my body tells me anyway.

We repeated the "bus into town" procedure, which was working very well but did mean that, when we reached the centre, we were miles from where we were actually meant to be. It was becoming apparent that the festival venues were very far apart from each other, but both of us were in the mood for walking, so we trudged for nearly ninety minutes to our destination, which was a bar called The Local. This was where the AMA Day Stage was situated. Rather like at South By Southwest, a day stage is where you can see all the artists who will be playing in the evening, but in less formal surroundings. In Austin, the Day Stage is a huge auditorium in the Convention Centre which holds at least a thousand people, but the performances tend to be very brief, fifteen minutes at most. Here in Nashville, as we discovered, it was the opposite. The Day Stage was in a tiny, cramped room, but musically was extremely attractive because the artists all played full sets of 45 minutes or more, sponsored by a local radio station. It was, therefore, by far the best place to be during the day, but you had to plan your tactics carefully.

Crammed into the sweltering room were several hundred mainly middle-aged people, but the set-up was by no means ideal for live music. The stage was very low, set into a corner and in front of it, for some reason, they had erected those chest-level tables and high stools that you find in bars. The people occupying these, I can only assume, must have arrived early in the morning, because they had plonked themselves down and set up camp for the entire day, rather like people sometimes do with blankets at outdoor festivals. This gave them the authority (in their minds) to tap on the shoulder anybody who had the audacity to stand in front of them. It meant that the only place Paul and I could stand, if we actually wanted to see the bands, was at the side of the stage, in front of a corridor leading through to the bathrooms. The artists themselves had no changing facilities, so also would be pushing past if they wanted to go to the loo. No chance of putting on airs and graces for them. This was, however, quite exciting for us as spectators.

The music was fantastically rewarding on this day. Many years ago, I became a big fan of Canadians Luke Doucet and Melissa McClelland, a married couple and duo of extraordinary beauty, musical ability and coolness, who came and played for us a couple of times in Winchester. We'd seen them numerous times in Austin but I'd been quite taken aback when they suddenly started using backing tracks and programmed effects, something which I felt completely changed their character. Plus, they changed their name to Whitehorse, about which I have the same reservations as I did about John Smith, i.e. if you google them you get hundreds of other white horses. What a joy it was to be able to comprehensively eat my words, as they stormed the little stage with a full band and rocked out in the most spectacular manner. As a bonus, they both recognised us from the stage and nodded in acknowledgement. I have to tell you that being nodded to by such cool people is quite thrilling.

There was more to come, arguably even better. A famous Texan musician called Alejandro Escovedo had put out a superb album themed around the subject of immigration, and teamed up with some Italian musicians who I actually knew. Antonio Gramentieri, affectionately known as Grammo, had visited us before in various formats, including backing Richard Buckner and Dan Stuart of Green On Red. Birgit and I had had the most wonderful experience of visiting him in his home town of Modigliana in Northern Italy. How exciting it was to see his work with Alejandro suddenly being recognised and increasing in popularity.

Currently known as Don Antonio, our friend shares the stage with various Italian pals, including the extraordinary Dennis. By trade, Dennis is a truck driver, driving bulk tankers full of red wine around the

Italian autostradas. He is also alarmingly lascivious and extremely funny. He therefore suits the rock and roll lifestyle down to the ground. Both of them are extremely tactile in a way that we English don't tend to be, although, to be fair, as soon as I reach America I start cuddling everyone in sight. The embraces that took place as they left the stage and recognised me were uniquely sweat-ridden but 100 percent sincere. The performance had been quite magical: full scale in-your-face rock and roll but with a potent message. This was what I had come to Nashville for and I couldn't possibly have been happier. We hung out in the sweltering backyard with the purple-haired granny who was compèring on behalf of the radio station.

The next job was to try and find something to eat. The Local did offer food but it was mainly of the type that gives me so many problems in America, i.e. stodgy burgers, greasy fries and dodgy looking bits of chicken anatomy.

"Don't worry," said Paul, "over there I can see a Chinese restaurant. It's part of a chain, but they are really good quality and I've been to one before."

This turned out to be a shocking waste of time, considering that we were in considerable haste to get to a record company showcase in town. First, we waited at the bar for nearly an hour, cringingly attempting to make conversation with a redneck couple who had done the "Where you from?" bit, and we couldn't escape because there was nowhere else to go. Then we were shown to a table and had to wait for nearly another hour until we eventually gave up, rather unfairly taking out our frustration on a probably innocent waitress.

"I'll show them," said Paul.

"What are you going to do?" I asked.

"I'm going to post on Twitter what a shocking experience we've just had. They hate that sort of thing and will probably give us a voucher for a free meal."

As it turned out, as far as I could tell, not a single person reacted to the tweet.

As it was so late, we had to take an Uber to the Cannery complex, where the record company showcase turned out to be definitely worth visiting, purely on account of a UK trio called William The Conqueror. This band is fronted by an ex-solo artist called Ruarri Joseph. I had seen them before, but they had transformed themselves into a really lively band with some impressive grooves. I also did something that was to happen again and again during the week, which was bumping into someone I knew, saying, "I can't talk now, it's too noisy. We'll catch up in a minute" and never seeing them again. In this case, it was Australian singer Emily Barker, who lives in Stroud, the town where I grew up.

Once again using the navigation device on Paul's phone, we headed for Jack White's Third Man building, mainly because I wanted to see it, but also because a Nashville singer called Erin Rae was due to perform, which she did with a degree of nervousness that added an extra edge to the show. It was a very hipster place with white walls, floor and ceiling, not particularly rock and roll.

We were both wilting through malnutrition but had noticed that there were various little restaurants very near our hotel, so we remounted the bus and tried the Mexican one. Here we had a very interesting conversation with the waitress. She explained, unprompted, that she was from Argentina and that she didn't have a work permit or a residence permit but wasn't concerned, because she didn't see how anybody would find her. There was no alcohol licence here, so we flushed down the delicious and quite spicy food with copious jugs of tap water. We must have had honest faces for her to tell us such information without fear of being shopped. In general, it had been pretty much the sort of day I had been hoping for on this trip.

As the "breakfast then back to bed" ritual had worked so well, there was a repeat of it the following morning before once again heading into town by bus. It was to be a day of Ubers from one venue to another, with most of the time again spent at the Day Stage. With artists of the calibre of the Milk Carton Kids and Richard Thompson, how could you say no?

I had first come across Richard Thompson in 1978, when I interviewed him and the rest of Fairport Convention for the university magazine at UEA. That was the day Sandy Denny told me to fuck off, a story that has still got plenty of mileage in it to this very day. To be stage-side, literally inches away from such a genius as Thompson, was a mind-blowing experience. It was possible to see all the lines on his face, but sadly not possible to work out whether he's got any hair under his beret. When I first met him, he had Shirley Temple locks of the calibre of Marc Bolan. He's actually quite an intimidating character in some ways, so I deemed it unlikely that he would appreciate me asking him whether he remembered meeting me in 1978. He chose to play on the side of the stage where we were standing, so it was possible to marvel at his extraordinarily intricate guitar playing. The fact that he played Meet On The Ledge made it even more emotional. Having only seen him on big stages, it was odd and exhilarating that he, too, had to push past us to get to his microphone. Shows like this are great levellers.

In the evening, we ended up at a pleasant venue called Douglas Corner, where our new friend Josh O'Keefe was hosting an open mic session which he was headlining. I must say I was impressed that someone so young had been brave enough to emigrate to a foreign country in order to make his fortune. It was a bit Dick-Whittington-like. As far as I can understand, he's living pretty much in penury in a tumbledown shack somewhere, but he has the vital sense of self-belief required.

Unfortunately, we had arrived too early and the afternoon show had not yet finished. This consisted of eight (count 'em) substandard musicians lined up across the stage and inflicting their turgid self-penned songs on each other and us, interspersed with telling each other how wonderful they were. I'm not a fan of open mic sessions. Maybe you might stumble across a superstar of the future but it's never been my experience, and I would prefer it if they did their rehearsals in front of a mirror in their bedrooms instead.

The last music of the day took place in a church. Now I know that churches are the currently cool places for acoustic gigs, but personally I don't find them either comfortable or relaxing. You always have to sit on stiff upright chairs, you're lucky if there's any booze and normally the sound is shit. All these applied in this case, but nonetheless it was fun to listen to Max Gomez, who not only is dramatically underrated but also gave me a free CD. I had to leave when he was approached by someone who had clearly mistaken him for someone else, with the resulting conversation therefore turning out to be excruciatingly embarrassing. Paul and I sought and found food in one of those establishments where there is a range of different outlets. This particular place was completely empty apart from us and the food was crap.

Saturday was Paul's last day. Both of us had given up on breakfast by this stage, and after a long lie-in, we headed back to Douglas Corner, because Paul had managed to leave his credit card there. I'd have been having a nervous breakdown if it had been me, but Paul didn't seem bothered at all, and indeed the proprietor had found it and returned it with a smile.

So off we went for a final time to the Day Stage. Here we took up a different position, because the stars were not quite so big and therefore there was more room to move. The music from the Band Of Heathens and the quite extraordinary Cordovas was of exceptionally high quality. The latter band specialised in numbers lasting about 90 seconds each and blending into each other, something I'd only ever seen before from Canadian band The Sadies.

It was now time to seek out something called the

Filming Stage. It didn't seem to be on any maps but we found it by walking a few miles and making some intelligent guesses as to where it might be. It wasn't open yet, which led to both of us inadvertently getting drunk for the first and only time of the week. We pottered about until we found a cheap Mexican chain joint which was doing two-for-one margaritas. We both did the special offer twice and felt as high as if we had taken some kind of drugs. I do know that we had a deep and meaningful conversation but I can't remember what it was about.

When Paul and I spend time in America, much of it passes in a state of hysteria. His British-style sense of irony has remained intact, which means that much of what we discuss could easily be interpreted by the casual listener as being deeply offensive. Because Paul has lived in America for nearly two decades, he's taken on aspects of American pronunciation and vocabulary which do sound odd but strangely endearing, because he has retained his English accent. Much mirth can be obtained from conversations along the lines of "It is an hon-ore to be enjoying the flay-vore of the liqu-ore in this neighb-ore-hood."

American vocabulary, as we all know, can cause

confusion. I always receive baffled looks when asking for the toilet, for example. I should, of course, have said either "bathroom" or "restroom". Normally, after a few days, I do remember to do so, even though the place in question neither contains a bath nor offers anywhere to rest. The delightful use of the word "trunk" to describe the boot of a car always brings to mind dear old Nellie The Elephant packing her trunk and saying goodbye to the circus.

I have one particular friend who takes great delight in taking American visitors to English pubs, simply so that she can suggest that they order some faggots. This is indeed an unusual word. In English, it can mean either an unspeakably disgusting blob of unidentified meat on a plate or, even more strangely, a bundle of wood to be carried on the back of a peasant, such as is depicted on the cover of the album "Led Zeppelin IV". In the US, however, it is a derogatory word for a gay person, often abbreviated to fag. I quickly learnt that it was inadvisable to refer to fag ends when complaining about litter.

Other popular and easy-to remember pieces of essential vocabulary include "sidewalk" (pavement) and "elevator" (lift), while ordering some "chips" always causes disappointment, because you'll merely be given a few crisps. My parents, when I was a child, once hosted a couple of American students, and I can remember my mother being shocked when their request for her to wash out a few pairs of "pants" resulted in her having to struggle to squeeze several pairs of denim jeans through the mangle.

Driving round Nashville, it seemed that, every few metres, there was some kind of delay caused by a "wreck". To my mind, this means a stately galleon stranded on rocks off the Cornish coast, but here it is a more prosaic car crash. Sometimes it is a mere dent or scratch, which makes the word "wreck" seem rather hyperbolic.

In fact, the Filming Stage turned out to be one of the most pleasant venues we visited, because it had a quite shady courtyard and lawn, where the stage had been set up. There was also free food, but it didn't suit Paul because there was nothing vegan. I stuffed myself with mac and cheese, which was not a very healthy thing to do. I really must stop indulging in things unnecessarily, simply because they are free.

On stage was a fantastic guitarist from Texas called Jesse Dayton. I proceeded to embarrass myself twice, first by rushing up to the drummer after the set, assuming he would recognise me from a gig they had done in Winchester. Of course he didn't, and I then made things worse by insisting on posing for a selfie with Jesse, even though it was quite clear he thought this was a supremely uncool thing to do, especially as he was in the middle of a discussion with a British agent who was trying to book him for a festival. I retreated, tail between legs, and we set off to a place called the Hi-Watt, which was part of the dreaded Cannery complex.

This was where I wanted to really impress Paul with an act he had never seen. Sarah Borges is a uniquely sassy rock and roller from Boston whom I absolutely adore, and I was certain we were going to have a wonderful climax to the festival. It turned out she was playing with a different band to the one that I was used to and, although I still loved it, horror of horrors, Paul didn't, and decided he wanted to leave halfway through. It's really embarrassing when you big something up and the person you take along doesn't enjoy it, but that was how it was. Paul needed to get up early in the morning to start the long drive back to Tulsa, so we settled for an early night.

Now I was all alone in a strange town. How was that going to work out?

DRIVE-BY TRUCKER

I had big plans, but first it was time to try out the hotel swimming pool, another facility that I had paid for and so was damn well going to use. As it turned out, nobody else seemed to know the pool existed and I spent a happy hour in there completely on my own. This was probably the only healthy thing I'd done the entire week.

My plans entailed travelling around and, being now no longer able to rely on the skills of Paul, it was finally time to try and get my head round Uber. All week people had been laughing about my hesitancy.

"You want to go to such-and-such a place? Of course,

just get an Uber."

This wasn't as easy as everybody seemed to think, because I have a pay-as-you-go phone and therefore no access to the internet other than using Wi-Fi. Everyone else seemed to have set themselves up with special deals that allowed them to use their phones abroad, but that wouldn't work with pay-as-you-go. "Why don't you have a phone that has a contract?" they asked. The answer is that I'm not allowed one.

The story behind this goes back a few years. I had always used pay-as-you-go (because I hardly use my phone anyway) but, walking down Eastleigh High Street one day, I spotted a bargain offer in a shop for a phone contract. "The time has finally come," I thought, and entered the shop.

It all turned out to be quite humiliating. They were keen to sell me the phone, of course, and I filled in numerous forms to set it all up. Eventually, the young shop assistant called out in a very loud voice, "Sorry sir, you've been rejected. You can't have a contract because of your credit history." I could see all the people behind me in the queue nudging each other and sniggering.

"That silly old fool's obviously up to his ears in debt," they were thinking.

I must say I was absolutely mortified because, to my mind, I was probably one of the most creditworthy customers that had ever walked through their door. In that typically British way, I had been faithfully paying my mortgage for twenty-five years, thus owning a house outright and with a reasonable amount of savings, plus a pension, but as far as the credit agencies were concerned, I didn't exist. After making a few enquiries, I discovered that if you have never had any debts, you aren't on their files, and if you aren't on their files, they won't give you any credit. Not that I wanted any credit, of course. I merely wanted to set up something along the lines of a standing order, such as I have for paying gas, electricity and council tax. Anyway I had to slink out of that shop with my tail between my legs and stick with my trusty old phone.

Having taken further advice, I duly got myself a credit card, because I was told that, if you use a credit card and pay it off monthly, that establishes that you are creditworthy. I dutifully did exactly that thing for several years and recently had another dose of unpleasant medicine. My phone had a cracked screen, so I took it into Vodafone to see if they could replace it. Hardly able to control their mirth, they assured me that this would be impossible but recommended me to buy a new phone on a contract. They laughed when I said I'd been rejected before, saying, "Oh, don't worry, any teenager can come in here and get a contract, so you'll be fine." There was then another long rigmarole, which involved me actually buying the phone and paying for it for before they had checked my creditworthiness. Somehow, I knew exactly what was going to happen and indeed it did: "Oh, I'm sorry sir, you've been rejected. You don't have a credit record."

So that was why I was in Nashville without the means of ordering Ubers anywhere where there wasn't a Wi-Fi signal. I decided that it would be possible just to wait in the hotel foyer, using their Wi-Fi, until the car appeared. I'd seen how it all worked, and so duly downloaded the Uber app. I must say it really is very exciting the first time you see that sweet little tiny car heading towards you on your screen. Could this really be happening?

Indeed it was, and my driver halted in front of the hotel. Then it was simply a matter of quickly switching off the phone and climbing in. The only thing was that, if I were to use it again later in the day, I would always have to find somewhere that had Wi-Fi.

My destination was once again East Nashville and the afternoon turned out to be a total joy. Robyn Hitchcock is in a relationship with an Australian singer called Emma Swift. Emma is co-owner of what we would call a second-hand clothes store, but they call Anaconda Vintage. They had arranged an afternoon of live music, presumably partly to promote the shop, but also to raise money for a charity and just generally be a nice place to hang out. I knew that both Robyn and Emma were going to be playing, so it was an ideal destination. The shop (and I admit that I am not a fan of second-hand clothes shops at all) was quite delightful and the range of clothes massive and tasteful, including Western shirts, one of which I found irresistible. Foolishly, I decided to buy it later and when I returned it had gone, so I grabbed a similar one and made sure to buy it immediately.

Shortly after that, a record company owner arrived

with his wife, who promptly tried on a body-hugging dress. As it fitted so well, I enthused about it to her husband, whom I hoped to impress. Instead, he made it quite clear that he didn't at all approve of me apparently ogling his wife.

The music was happening in a little alleyway just outside the shop. It was drizzling, but they had built a sweet little canopy and every single performer was quite outstanding. Half way through the afternoon, Robyn and Emma did a few songs as a duo with beautiful harmonies, but the highlight for me was a completely unexpected and unscheduled performance by Nashville singer Caitlin Rose.

Originally from Dallas (the name of one of her most beautiful cover versions, written by Ian Felice of the Felice Brothers), she had grown up in a very Country environment in Nashville. Her father Johnny is a country music marketing manager, while her mother Liz is a renowned and very successful songwriter, who won a Grammy for her numerous co-writes with Taylor Swift. Caitlin herself began singing at the age of sixteen and was originally working in the punk genre. That was why I'd become such a fan of her music, which made her huge-lunged Country style much more spiky and challenging than so many of her contemporaries. I happened to know Spencer Cullum, her British pedal steel player, and for a couple of years had been trying to book her for a show. But, round about 2015, having been on a major label and released a great album called "The Go Between", she simply disappeared off the scene. So to suddenly see her shyly sitting on a stool in this slightly dingy alleyway, playing three songs to an audience of about fifteen people ... well, it got my old tear ducts threatening to misbehave.

I met another English guy there, who was a peripheral member of the gang that travels to Nashville each year for the AMA event, and he summoned an Uber to take us to another courtyard event down the road. This was considerably less enjoyable, even though the star names were bigger. There were long queues for everything and everybody was talking about a shooting that had taken place in the area the night before, which unnerved me slightly. Luckily, I found a bit of Wi-Fi and was able to summon a car to take me to my final destination of the week, a record store called Fond Object, where someone was playing who I really love. This was JD Wilkes, who used to be in an extraordinary band called Th' Legendary Shack Shakers. Their guitarist had the distinction of having an entire Gibson guitar tattooed onto his upper body, while Mr Wilkes, the lead singer, looked and behaved like a little rat, shinning up and down gantries and spitting a lot. Well, you had to be there, but he's a true entertainer and now a solo performer.

At Fond Object, I got into a conversation with two European agents from whom I book bands, and a rather rich guy who runs a festival in his stately home. I shared several IPA beers with them and was feeling warm and contented by the time I snuck into the record store to use their Wi-Fi for the last time. I was fed up of being on my own now by now and looking forward to the next day, because that was when Birgit was due to arrive.

Birgit is my wife, and now it's time for me to tell you something about her. We've been together for over forty years, having met when I was working in Germany and she was a seventeen-year-old sixth form student. For a slightly anxious person like me, Birgit is the perfect partner to have in my life. Nobody will be surprised that I think she is beautiful, but she also has numerous characteristics that make her the ideal life-sharer. She is calm, organised and reliable and has a cheerful willingness to join in with almost all the daft ideas I have. This makes her an exceptionally good person to have holidays with.

But there is a more practical reason for her being such a great companion on a trip like this. She can drive. She can drive very well indeed, either on the left or the right hand side of the road. This is essential for the two of us, because I unfortunately can't drive or, to make it clearer, I am physically able to drive but I'm mentally incapable of it. I have a driving phobia, which I shall now attempt to explain.

I can't wait for self-driven cars to become a reality. Sadly, I fear I won't live long enough to see the day when they will be safe enough to be unleashed on the roads, but even if I do, we can assume they will be priced to be accessible only to the super-rich. I have a reason for this dream. One day, I'd like to drive on a motorway again. The last time I did that was in 1976.

If you don't drive at all, no one thinks you are weird. But if you do drive but can't drive on motorways, you are considered to be very odd indeed. That's me.

It crops up in conversation a lot, because everyone knows I have this affliction. "I know," people say, "I hate motorways too". But that isn't the point. I don't just hate them, I live in such terror of them that I'm finding it painful just writing these sentences. My phobia is total. If a terrible emergency were to crop up tomorrow which made it vital for me to get onto the M3, for example to reach an airport because a relative was dying, I wouldn't be able to do it.

"Describe how you feel," people say. Well, I can tell you how it started. I used to drive on the Autobahn in Germany. I remember those huge trucks with trailers that would swing around in the inside lane. My wheezy old Beetle would struggle to overtake them. Sometimes it would take a minute or two of inching alongside them before the blessed relief of pulling in, and during that time, there would be angry BMW drivers in the mirror flashing their lights at me. But there was nowhere to go. Cars to the left of you, lorries to the right, stuck in the middle lane. It was claustrophobia in its most extreme form, but back then, I was able to cope with it. Most people wouldn't even think of it as an issue.

Those suffering from conventional claustrophobia are compelled to get out of their situations and normally, with a little embarrassment, they can. An elevator will normally stop eventually, a theatre will have an exit, even a cable car will reach the top of the mountain, but if you are driving on a motorway, there's no escape.

"What does it feel like?" people ask. In a kind way, they try to empathize. But they can't imagine what this phobia is like. I was first struck by it in 1976, on the way home from seeing the Rolling Stones at Knebworth. Surrounded by headlights at speed, I suddenly felt overwhelmed by confusion. Were the lights in front of me, behind me or in the mirror? How far away were they? I literally froze, having no control over my body or mind. I lost all understanding of how to drive the car. I had to stop, get away, but it was impossible. My head span, I felt sick, I couldn't see properly and my limbs were out of control.

It was a miracle I didn't crash and die there and then,

but the next day, assuming it must have been some weird one-off, I tried again. And it happened again, this time in daylight. And then again. There is a strong element of OCD in this. I don't believe that I won't plough into the nearest lorry, or that its driver won't have a heart attack and veer across the motorway. It could happen, and that is enough to convince my troubled mind that it will.

Already, my mind had taken over control of my intentions, learning the wrong responses, but I was determined not to be beaten by such nonsense. When I realised that something had to be done, I took medical advice, but before that, my dear wife offered to take me out on practice drives on dual carriageways. It was hopeless and we would always end up stranded at the first lay-by and she would have to drive me home as I shivered and sobbed.

Had my GP heard of this strange driving affliction? No, but he was sure it was merely stress and anxiety. He prescribed two sorts of pill, one of which I stopped almost immediately after I discovered it was an enormously strong and highly addictive anti-depressant.

The others were standard tranquillisers, to be taken before attempting to drive. Bafflingly, the label said that one should avoid driving after taking the pills. That was helpful. And significantly, the doctor asked me if I felt I could drive better after having consumed alcohol? I did. But it obviously wasn't a solution that it made sense to pursue.

I consulted a series of psychiatrists and psychotherapists. The first person I went to just made things worse. Despite his opulent house, his leather chaise-longue and the long series of letters after his name, he showed no sign of being able to relate to the condition. He also lived in a place only accessible via a busy road, so that didn't exactly help. Another one tried really hard to help me by coming out in the car with me, the idea being to overcome the phobia by confronting it. In theory, it was a sound approach, but after a couple of sessions, he was so shit-scared that he told me he didn't dare continue. I didn't blame him.

Yet another psychotherapist thought that group therapy might help. Unfortunately, the other participants had quite different phobias, of bats, mice and snakes.

They didn't empathise with my problem and I didn't empathise with theirs. Homeopathy wasn't any better. The white-coated expert was obviously a charlatan and sold me some pills, which I knew were made of sugar.

The most helpful person was a local acupuncturist, although it was a bit awkward. Her daughter, who was one of my pupils, kept walking in to find me spreadeagled on the couch, looking like a pin cushion. The acupuncturist also treated several of my friends and would regale me with information about their personal problems. I could only assume that she was also telling them all about mine. What she did do, however, was teach me good relaxation techniques, which I have found useful in a variety of situations ever since.

Finally, annoyed at my GP's insistence that there was nothing for it but to "keep taking the tablets", I changed to another doctor. He immediately said I should stop taking the tablets and also stop driving.

"Stop driving?"

"Why not? Millions of people don't drive. What's the big deal?"

He was right. I was reassured to look up several high-profile celebrities (such as Liam Gallagher and Ricky Gervais) and find that they had never driven and didn't care (although I guess they can afford chauffeurs).

I had long since accepted that I was to remain a non-motorway driver for the rest of my days when I was approached by the BBC, wanting to film a documentary item about my affliction. They already had an agenda in place. They would film me being treated by a hypnotist, an extraordinary lady I christened Mystic Meg. She would carry out a miracle cure, they would film me bowling along the M3 and they would have their programme. Of course it was a failure (although I really tried, as keen as anyone for an unexpected transformation) and they doctored some footage of me on a short piece of dual carriageway to make it seem like a success.

I now know that the only way to have conquered it was to have been forced, again and again, to confront it, but the unique nature of this problem made that impossible. I would never have been able to do it on my own, and no one else would ever have had the courage to accompany me. In my mind, I would certainly lose control and kill myself, my companion and numerous other drivers. That was too much of a risk to take.

I would love to know if I am the only person in the world who has this problem. When the programme went out, no one contacted the BBC saying they recognised the symptoms. I have met plenty of people who don't like driving on motorways but none who simply can't. Plus, recently, by an awful set of circumstances, I suddenly briefly found myself on a stretch of dual carriageway in Southampton. Was this the confrontation I needed? Was I cured? Nope, it was just as bad as the first time. I completely freaked and it is only the fact that there was practically no traffic that allowed me survive and be able to write this. No happy ending there, then.

Luckily, unlike some people with similar phobias, I am perfectly happy to be a passenger, largely because Birgit is such a good driver. Thus it was that I took an Uber to meet her at the airport and we proceeded straight to the car hire area, in order to pick up the vehicle we had ordered online. The lady at the car hire desk launched straight into, "Oh my god, I love your accent" mode and immediately said how much she loved England, even though she'd never been there. When I enquired how she could love it so much if she had never experienced it, she explained that it was entirely based on her passionate love for Ed Sheeran. When I told her that I'd promoted concerts by Ed Sheeran and once fallen asleep during one of them, she was slightly confused as to whether to cuddle me for having been in his presence or punch me for disrespecting him. I decided to pretend that I thought he was good, in case she took a knife to the brake pipes before handing over the vehicle.

We picked up the slightly battered white Kia and were given a piece of paper with a plan of the car, on which we were supposed to put a cross for each dent. As the bodywork consisted almost entirely of dents, this was quite a hard task, but the gentleman in the kiosk was remarkably casual, saying that they didn't really care about it anyway. This frightened me slightly, because I'd read numerous articles when people have had to pay thousands of pounds for damage to vehicles that they haven't actually caused, but the guy merely said, "Don't worry, we're not like that." We hoped that it would turn out to be true and temporarily banished it from our minds.

As Birgit had arrived late in the afternoon, we decided just to stay in the hotel and have a general catch-up. Next to the Mexican restaurant outside was also a pizza takeaway joint, so we grabbed a couple of those. In my case, I made the grave error of pouring two packets of chilli flakes all over mine, thus inducing much gasping and pouring of sweat not normally associated with pizza consumption. In the morning, we both entered the pool, which, rather upsettingly, also had some other guests in it, in the form of something you never like to see, namely overweight, lobster-like UK tourists. For some reason, all they did was bob around in the pool rather than actually using it for swimming purposes. One of the guys actually complimented me on my sporting prowess, even though I was merely doing my normal extremely slow and laboured breaststroke up and down. Nonetheless, a quick swim like this can make you feel fantastically good, especially on a hot day.

I managed to impress Birgit with my in-depth knowledge of the bus system and, in no time at all, we had been whisked into the centre. I had purposely not spent any time exploring the city because I wanted us to do that together. To this end, I had booked an open-top bus tour and, while we were waiting for it to arrive, we wandered along the riverfront a little bit. On the other side was the extraordinarily ugly Nissan stadium, while on the town side there was an attempt at a historical site, in the form of a wooden fort that you couldn't actually get into. Other American cities make a much better job of emphasising their heritage, but Nashville is so obsessed with the music scene that it seems to ignore everything else.

While waiting for the bus, we saw the fattest person that either of us had ever encountered. It was almost impossible not to gape. The worst thing was that she was sitting, overspilling two chairs, gasping for breath, with a huge bottle of coke in one hand a gigantic fat-dripping burger in the other. Now I'm fully aware that this is a fattist observation, but it really was impossible to ignore, and the only conclusion you could come to was that the peddlers of such crap really do have as much responsibility for the ill-health of their victims as the manufacturers of tobacco products.

The guide on the bus tour took us through the

history of Nashville. Originally an Indian settlement, predominantly Cherokee and Chickasaw, Nashville was founded in 1779, and was originally called Fort Nashborough. The city quickly grew as a river port, and later as a railway centre. By 1843, Nashville had become the capital of the state of Tennessee, but it suffered badly in the Civil War. In the late 19th century, the city gained a level of prosperity which lasts to this day, with high-tech companies relocating in droves and huge building programmes everywhere. These moves are generally not welcomed by the impoverished musicians who have traditionally inhabited the city.

It was in 1925 that Nashville took its first steps towards becoming "Music City USA", with the founding of the Grand Ole Opry, which became the world's longest-running radio programme. The 1940s saw the advent of music publishing as a major industry in Nashville, with various record companies and music publishers today still having their world headquarters in the city.

The emphasis back then was on R & B, with the Everly Brothers, Roy Orbison and even Jimi Hendrix playing on Jefferson Street. By the 1950s, the emphasis had moved firmly to Country music and the Country Music Association was formed to promote it. Despite the prominence of the Johnny Cash Museum in Nashville, Cash himself never lived there, although he did record prolifically in Columbia Studios in the city and, of course, performed regularly on the Grand Ole Opry.

In more modern days, Bob Dylan recorded three albums in the city, including Nashville Skyline, opening the doors for Joan Baez, Neil Young and others to gravitate to Tennessee's studios. Nowadays, Jack White has his Third Man studio in Nashville, and acts like Kings Of Leon and Taylor Swift continue the momentum, which is largely dominated by the current wave of commercial country artists like Garth Brooks, the world's biggest-selling solo artist.

Other than all this useful information, the bus tour duly revealed that Nashville doesn't really have much to recommend it from an architectural point of view. The State Capitol is nondescript and the only building to create any excitement is a surprising model of the Parthenon, which adorns the Centennial Park. Originally built for Tennessee's 1897 Centennial Exposition, this edifice is no Spinal Tap-style Stonehenge. It is in fact a full-size replica. It actually does have a purpose, which is to house the city's main art gallery.

The trip did at least help us to get our bearings for a later ramble round "downtown". We bought a fridge magnet from a souvenir shop and managed to survive for about fifteen minutes in one of the music bars, listening to a band murdering various country classics. It consisted of some of the aspiring young musicians who gravitate to Nashville, because of its thriving live scene, with ample chances to collaborate with like-minded musicians on songwriting projects. They "pay their dues" by playing endless shifts of covers in tacky tourist bars and living on tips. We did put some money in the tip jar, of course – the etiquette very much demanded it and besides, we felt sorry for them.

In the huge Convention Centre, we spent over an hour searching for something called the Songwriters' Hall Of Fame. This actually turned out to be an oversized bookcase in a lobby at the bottom of a flight of stairs, but it did have a good exhibit about Townes van Zandt. We had agreed not to bother with the probably considerably larger Country Music Hall Of Fame, since neither of us is particularly bothered about Country music and we knew we would be spending a lot of time in museums in the coming weeks. The day was completed by a third visit (for me) to the Bakersfield restaurant, which I enjoyed immensely but Birgit liked less, on account of the food being too spicy for her taste. A couple of gorgeous margaritas made up for that.

On the way in, my bus expertise had let me down to the extent that I absent-mindedly put a twenty-dollar bill into the machine, forgetting that it didn't give change. We were therefore in possession of a ticket that still had about fifteen dollars' worth of credit. At the bus stop we found an obviously destitute lady who had been asking people for change to help with her bus fare. We naturally gave her the ticket, explaining that it still had value, and she duly used it on the bus. But of any thanks there was no hint. To be fair, she seemed to be in such a drugged-up state that she probably had little empathy left.

The next morning, it was time for our road trip to begin. Birgit had brought our Sat Nav with her and we had upgraded it to work in America, so we headed straight for our first port of call, the utterly delightful Loveless Café, which was situated near the start of the Natchez Trace Parkway, on which we planned to spend the next couple of days. Originally a small and insignificant motel, the café is now quite a tourist attraction and is surrounded by souvenir shops and the like. It had opened in 1951, we discovered, when proprietors Lon and Annie Loveless started serving fried chicken and "biscuits" to passing motorists on Highway 100, initially served at picnic tables on their front porch. But their food became so popular that they converted their home into a restaurant and built a motel next door. Annie continued making her signature biscuits and preserves in the kitchen.

We entered and waited for a table to become available, studying the hundreds of photos on the walls of Country stars who have eaten at the café. We weren't particularly hungry and so observed with quite some anticipation some small scones which adorned plates on every table, accompanied by little tubs of jam (or "jelly", as the Americans call it). It looked like something along the lines of a cream tea, exactly what we would like.

When we eventually were allocated a table, we were surprised to find these items nowhere on the menu. Our friendly young student waiter Brad explained that these were, in fact, the "biscuits" and were a starter, given free to every customer.

As it looked like an ideal meal for a small appetite, we asked if it was possible just to have biscuits and some coffee. He was absolutely astonished and, I think, slightly offended, but took it all in his stride. Thus we ended up having a nice "afternoon tea", complete with numerous refills, for the price of a couple of cups of coffee. But Brad was right: all around us, we could observe people scoffing first the plate of biscuits, then a gigantic main course and finally a huge dessert. No wonder most of the customers looked seriously in need of a drastic diet.

TRACE ELEMENT

Just a few metres from the door of the Loveless Café, we found the beginning of the Natchez Trace Parkway. I had been particularly looking forward to this because, if you have a driving phobia, you frankly don't enjoy hurtling down six-lane highways, whereas I anticipated that the Natchez Trace Parkway would be a considerably quieter proposition, and so it transpired. It was practically entirely without traffic. We would sometimes drive three or four miles without seeing a single car.

The Parkway is completely free of all the things you expect to find on American roads. For a start, there are no houses, no shops, no hoardings, no bars, no restaurants, no hotels and there is an upper speed limit of 40 miles an hour. The road ambles peacefully through beautiful countryside and is the motorised equivalent of a pleasant country walk. It stretches 450 miles and was completed in 2005.

The idea for the Natchez Trace Parkway was conceived in the 1930s. The route set up was to follow the old Natchez Trace as closely as possible. The Trace had been a major foot trail in the 1700s and then became one of America's first National Roads. It went from Nashville to Natchez, which were both towns of strategic and commercial importance. From 1699 to 1763, the entire area had been controlled by France. After the Seven Years' War, France gave the majority of its North American land to Spain and the Mississippi River became the border between the English and Spanish colonies. Navigation of the river was shared by both countries. The French had built a fort at Natchez in 1716. By the time the Spanish took control, the town had grown into a major commercial centre.

Goods needed to be transported down the Mississippi

in the era before the railways. Although this was easy when going downstream, travelling upstream against the current was impossible. Boatmen heading for New Orleans therefore sold their barges for scrap once they reached their destination. The only way back home was to walk, and the trail they created to walk along was the Natchez Trace.

The Trace began as a series of disjointed Indian trails that connected the Natchez area to what would become Nashville. Gradually, the Indian paths became one well-worn, continuous trail. It took about six weeks to travel to Nashville on foot, or roughly four by horse.

After the Revolution, Spain took control of the Mississippi River and closed the port of New Orleans to American goods. In 1795, the dispute was finally resolved by the Treaty of Madrid. After this treaty, the Mississippi was open to tax-free travel by American merchants, and the Natchez area was given to the United States. In 1798, the area was organized into what was called the Mississippi Territory.

The government decided to expand the Natchez Trace into a National Road. Treaties were signed with the

Chickasaw and Choctaw Indians and the Trace began to expand. Previously only used by boat people traffic, the road now started being used for general travel. However, it could be quite dangerous for travellers, as bandits abounded, as well as deep mud, mosquitoes, poison ivy and poisonous snakes in the swamps. Of course, white and Indian businessmen soon began to set up "stands," or inns, along the Trace to offer accommodation and sustenance to tired and hungry travellers. Only one stand remains today, at Mount Locust, but as you travel along the Parkway, you can see signs marking where stands used to be.

Today's route largely follows the original Trace and every couple of miles there is an excuse to stop. Small car parks by the road lead to historic sites, walking trails, scenic overlooks and nature trails. At some stages there are even opportunities to go off-road and drive along the original Trace as it was before it was developed as a tourist route. This really gives you a feel what it would have been like for those original travellers. I thought I'd died and gone to heaven when we reached a particular nature trail where there was no sign of any other human beings and we saw numerous tiny hummingbirds, plus a couple of deer, and sat for nearly an hour watching two beavers repeatedly traversing a lake, while transporting pieces of wood to create their dam. I'm afraid to say I had a little weep. As we emerged from the woods, we met two ladies who were armed with a forked stick, to ward off, they informed us, the numerous venomous snakes to be found in the area. Good thing we hadn't known that before.

Another fascinating detour was to a mysterious memorial to Captain Meriwether Lewis, near Grinder's Stand. As personal secretary to Thomas Jefferson, Lewis was sent on an expedition to Louisiana and later became governor of the Upper Louisiana Territory. While travelling to Washington, where some of his bills had been queried, he passed along part of the Natchez Trace. On the morning of October 11 1809, while staying in Grinder's Stand, Lewis died of gunshot wounds. Most evidence suggests that Lewis' wounds were self-inflicted, and it was generally accepted that he must have committed suicide, but some later accounts suggested that Lewis might have been murdered. It's one of the most eerily atmospheric places on the Trace.

We pulled off the road repeatedly into deserted car parks and everywhere we went was pure fascination. We followed a trail down to Jackson Falls, which turned out to have no water in them, on account of the drought-like conditions. The weather, of course, continued to be utterly idyllic throughout. At the Falls, we met an unlikely group of roadies - young bearded students clad in black shorts and T-shirts saying "Crew". They were so out of condition that they were suffering from exhaustion, having walked the mere mile or so from the previous car park.

When researching where to stay along the Trace, it wasn't easy to find any accommodation, because there are no hotels anywhere near it, so I'd had to choose a particular town to head for. We had agreed that we were going to book accommodation in advance as much as possible, because of so many bad experiences, many years ago, of trying to find hotels in France late at night and discovering that they were all booked up or closed. This causes stress, and the idea of this road trip was to avoid stress as far as possible, so I had stuck a pin in a map and come up with Waynesborough. This was chosen simply because I liked the name and could imagine John Wayne, pistols cocked, striding into the saloon for a shoot-out.

The motel I had picked looked gorgeous and indeed, to be fair, the photo on the booking website hadn't been doctored, but merely been taken from an extremely advantageous angle. What looked like a country mansion on the website was a standard motel by the side of a busy road, overlooking an industrial estate. But the Indian owner, having reacted with the customary amazement at the suggestion that we might want to walk into town, did recommend us a particular restaurant. Pretty much all the franchisees of all the motels we visited were charming Indians (Indian Indians, not Native American Indians), which was unexpected but very pleasant. He said the restaurant was on the square, which slightly baffled me because small American towns seldom have squares.

Waynesboro did indeed have a square at its heart. Most of the shops round it were abandoned but there was one restaurant, which was adjacent to one of the few other functioning buildings, which inevitably was the local headquarters of the Republican Party. The meal began with an awful shock, which we received when ordering from the friendly young teenage waitress:

"Two burgers and two beers please."

"We don't have beer."

"You don't have beer?!"

"No sir, this is a dry county. You can have water, Cola or Dr Pepper."

This was bad news indeed, as we were both parched and both hate sugary drinks, but as there were no other restaurants in town, we settled for water. At the table next to us, a very stiff meal was taking place. A father was clearly having a scheduled meeting with his estranged children, all of whom largely ignored their very full plates and stared at their phones for the entire evening.

Back at the hotel, it was time to indulge in that familiar American experience of trying to find anything whatsoever worth tuning into on TV. In the unlikely event that there is anything worth watching, it's only a matter of a couple of minutes before it will be interrupted by advertisements, mainly for strange and incomprehensible pharmaceutical items whose merits are entirely negated by the enormous list of terrifying-sounding side effects, which lasts much longer than the actual advertisement. But it had been a long and wonderful day and, having given up hope of ever finding out the results of the US equivalent of "Dragon's Den", we slept like logs. The following day's target was Muscle Shoals.

As we crossed the state line from Tennessee to Alabama, I'd been searching for a generic way to describe the Natchez Trace parkway. There's a road in Southern Germany called the Romantic Road. It is indeed extremely romantic, but even it has the odd town here and there, whereas the Natchez Trace Parkway simply glides on calmly for hundreds of miles without touching any agglomerations. As far as I'm concerned, it's so perfect that it should be christened the Idyllic Road.

On the route towards Muscle Shoals, we were attracted by a place called Florence. Having spent pleasant times in its Italian namesake, we had high hopes for this town, but it turned out to be a major disappointment. We spent nearly two hours searching for anything of any interest whatsoever, all the while panicking about whether we had understood the parking restrictions correctly. What the Americans call "historic" does not equate with European notions of the concept. Still, we did have quite a nice ice cream in a sweltering parlour in the largely abandoned main street.

There was a reason for heading for the Muscle Shoals recording studios. Not only did The Rolling Stones record several tracks of their classic album "Sticky Fingers" there, but it was also the source of one of my favourite records of all time, namely "Shoot Out At The Fantasy Factory", by Traffic. This album was the follow-up to the very highly acclaimed "Low Spark Of High Heeled Boys" and, while most people claim that the latter was a greater record, I prefer "Shoot Out". It was very clearly the product of gargantuan drug use, being almost entirely snail-paced and highly stoned in character, but the musicianship is sublime and one reason for that is the presence of the session musicians known as the Swampers.

The studio was originally opened by them in 1969. Then known as the Muscle Shoals Rhythm Section, the

Swampers consisted of Jimmy Johnson on guitar, David Hood on bass, Barry Beckett on keyboards and Roger Hawkins on drums. They had got together at the Fame studio in Muscle Shoals (which is just down the road and can also be visited). At Fame, the Swampers had became renowned for accompanying artists like Etta James, Aretha Franklin and Wilson Pickett, in a style of funky soul/R&B. In 1969, the Swampers decided to branch out on their own and open their own studio at 3614 Jackson Highway. It was very unusual at the time for musicians to actually own their own recording studio and administer all aspects themselves. From working with him at Fame, they already had a good relationship with Jerry Wexler, the boss of Atlantic Records, and he was willing to lend them money to buy equipment.

The studio got off to a great start, producing Cher's first solo album, which actually bore the title "3614 Jackson Highway" and has a photo of the building on its cover. Also that year, they recorded an album with Lulu called "New Routes". Unlikely as it may seem, this is a great record, one of the many now displayed on the walls of the studio's basement. It followed a trend set by

Dusty Springfield, who, the year before, had made the album "Dusty In Memphis" with American soul session musicians.

Muscle Shoals Studio's first chart success came in 1969 with a one-off hit by RB Greaves, called "Take A Letter Maria". Just at the same time, the Rolling Stones took over the studio for three nights, during which they recorded "You Gotta Move", "Wild Horses" and "Brown Sugar", all of which eventually appeared on their 1971 album "Sticky Fingers". The sessions, which have since passed into legend, were slotted, at the suggestion of Keith Richards, into a few days off that had been built into the Stones' US tour. The band felt it was an appropriate place to record "You Gotta Move", as it had been written by Mississippi Fred McDowell. "Wild Horses", in particular, captured the swampy feel of the Deep South area they found themselves in.

In the nine years from 1969 to 1978, the Swampers played on over two hundred records, of which more than seventy-five went Gold or Platinum. Artists who recorded at the studio included Lynyrd Skynyrd ("Sweet Home Alabama"), Bob Dylan, Simon and Garfunkel,

Cat Stevens and Rod Stewart. Eventually, by 1978, the studio had outgrown its premises and therefore moved to a larger building nearby. Original Swamper David Hood (who is the father of Drive By Truckers' Patterson Hood) hit the road with Traffic for several years and is still an active musician.

Following closure, the original location on Jackson Highway was used first as an electrical goods retailer and later as an appliance repair shop, before falling into disrepair in the late 1990s. It lay empty until being reopened in 2009 as a working studio, where the Black Keys recorded their album "Brothers". In recent years, it has finally been restored to its former glory by a music foundation, recognising its heritage and potential as a cultural tourist attraction. Bizarrely, but happily, this was largely achieved with the help of a large donation from Beats Electronics, the audio company owned by Dr Dre.

The hotel I had booked was a so-called Red Roof Inn. This was a chain of which we had previously had no experience, but which turned out to be exactly the same as any Days Inn, Motel 6 or Super 8, which was fine. It even had a tiny pool, which we leapt into with alacrity. We then programmed the address of Muscle Shoals Studio into our admittedly slightly fallible Sat Nav and set off. In the middle of a large metal bridge crossing the Tennessee River, our friendly digital guide announced, "You have reached your destination."

"This can't possibly be right," said Birgit, so we pulled over at the first opportunity and re-programmed it. The result was exactly the same. As we crossed the bridge in the opposite direction, it once more announced that we were where we were wanting to be. Several more attempts produced the same result, so all we could think of doing was returning to the hotel and asking for advice. The previously rather grumpy receptionist burst into a wide smile; this was obviously something that she had had to deal with many times before.

"That would be because Muscle Shoals studio isn't in Muscle Shoals," she announced triumphantly. "Did you put Muscle Shoals into your GPS?"

"Yes, of course I did. It's called Muscle Shoals, isn't it?"

"Ah, but that's where you're wrong. Muscle Shoals studio is not in Muscle Shoals. It's in Sheffield."

It's always slightly baffling when you come across the names of English towns and cities in America. We had already passed a Gloucester, a Worcester, a Winchester and a Manchester, so it wasn't really much of a surprise to find ourselves near Sheffield. A quick bit of Sat Nav manipulation, replacing Muscle Shoals by Sheffield, led us to our destination, the tiny nondescript white building we had been seeking at number 3614, Jackson Highway.

It seemed likely that we had misunderstood the promise on the website that there would be hourly tours, as the place appeared to be deserted. But no, as we entered, we found a small gift shop and a couple of friendly staff. Before long, we had been joined by two or three middle-aged couples rather like ourselves. We all fitted the expected demographic to a tee (the men being overawed and the wives shoulder-shruggingly tolerant), and set off with our guide, Chase, for what turned out to be one of the most emotional experiences of my life.

First, we entered the basement, which was where the musicians would hang out when not recording. It was decorated from top to bottom with sleeves of albums that had been recorded there, classics from the likes of

Lynyrd Skynyrd, Bob Seger, Traffic, the Rolling Stones, of course, plus Rod Stewart and Cat Stevens. Also in the cellar was a secret bar. Sheffield having been in those days a dry county, the only way bands like the Stones could get their hands on any alcohol was to send someone out to the next county to smuggle a few crates back and hide them in this wood-panelled cave, which was always kept locked.

Upstairs in the studio, which is a working recording facility, was where the real excitement began. Following decades of intermittent dereliction, the building had only been reopened for visitors six months before. What's so brilliant about Muscle Shoals is that you don't just look at the studio, you are allowed to be a part of it, playing the instruments (including the piano that Jim Dickinson played on "Wild Horses") and touching the equipment, for all the world as if you were recording there yourself. The tour is, of course, illustrated by iconic pieces of music that were created there, and among the many exhibits is the invoice for 1009 dollars presented to the Rolling Stones for when they recorded "Wild Horses".

Chase told us the story of how the Stones locked

Keith Richards into the tiny toilet with the melody for the track and instructed him not to emerge until he'd written the lyrics, which he duly did. We do not know what else Keith did in the toilet, but I made sure to go in and take a selfie in there.

I quizzed Chase about the making of "Shoot Out At The Fantasy Factory". Apparently, Traffic did not have the requisite work permits to record in the USA at all, and the whole process had to be carried out in some secrecy. He smiled conspiratorially when I enquired what he knew about their legendarily copious drug intake. As we left, Birgit took my photo on the small balcony where people like the Stones would go out for fresh air or to smoke something or other. It just felt so surreal and so perfect that I'm afraid to say I burst into tears.

We had been puzzling about where to go out for dinner, because all that was to be seen along any of the roads were chains such as McDonald's, Burger King, Taco Bell, etc, etc, none of which held any attraction at all. I button-holed Chase and described what we were after: something authentic, something local that wasn't a chain, something where we could relax with a beer and possibly some music.

Chase said, "I know just the place. All you need to do is turn left down this road and at the end of it you'll find Champy's." This turned out to be a spectacularly good piece of advice, because Champy's was everything I had dreamed of when I made the request: a wooden road house specialising in locally sourced fried chicken. Normally chicken has no attraction for me, but everybody I had spoken to in advance of the trip said you had to try fried chicken if you were in the south of America. The waitress was absolutely charming and amazed by our presence, because it was not the sort of place that tourists would normally find.

Personally, I have absolutely no problem with standards of service in the USA. If people are being nice to us just because they want a good tip, that suits me just fine, because I like people who are nice to me. We had a few questions about the menu, for example what Hush Puppies were. She couldn't really describe them, so suggested giving us a couple to try. They turned out to be something along the lines of falafels, extremely tasty and easy to eat. I had already noticed with great joy that the cold beer was just three dollars a pint and in the end, we both went for the fried chicken. This was a perfect choice, because it was the best chicken I have ever eaten in my life: gigantic hunks of breast meat in spicy breadcrumbs that luckily were so tender that even the flimsy plastic cutlery provided was just about able to cut them.

As we returned to the Red Roof Motel, feeling suitably replete, I did notice that the next door room had a couple of picnic chairs and some stuff that looked suspiciously like drug paraphernalia outside it, but it was none of our business, so we thought no more about it. We were asleep by ten, but around about midnight, the noise started. It was two people sitting in those chairs, accompanied by a dog, loud music and endless loud, coarse and profane chatter.

Despite the inconvenience, my overwhelming thought was "guns" and I was confident that Birgit's earplugs would be protecting her from the disturbance. Thus it was with a certain amount of horror that I became aware that she had got out of bed, wrapped herself in her sheet and was striding determinedly towards the door.

"For God's sake, you'll get us shot," I whispered as loudly as I dared.

"Nonsense, I'm going to sort them out," she replied and, before I could protest any further, had wrenched the door open and was lecturing the pair in a very polite but clear way on the selfishness of depriving other guests of their sleep.

"That's it," I thought. "I'm going to be pulling her out of a pool of blood any moment now," but I was wrong. A deathly hush descended and we were able to drift back into undisturbed slumber for the rest of the night. In the morning, there was no sign of our neighbours and, by a miracle, we were still alive.

TUPELO HONEY

The next state line on the Trace was between Alabama and Mississippi. We were heading for Tupelo, Mississippi, but a couple of weeks before we were due to leave, we received a very strange message from the owner of the airbnb that we had booked there. Basically, she said that she had had a baby and therefore it wouldn't be convenient to have guests. You'd have thought it might have been something that she would have considered earlier, but maybe she was one of those over-confident prospective parents who assume that having a child will make no difference to their lives. Either way, we were suddenly without anywhere to stay in Tupelo.

"Why don't you stay with my parents?" suggested an American-born friend of ours. As time was short, we asked our friend to email his father and, before we knew it, we had booked ourselves in to visit the parents. Now the day had come to meet them, but first, on the final stretch (for now) of the Natchez Trace Parkway, we visited the Chickasaw Village site and spent a couple of hours in the very informative Trace Visitor Centre at milepost 266, just outside Tupelo. The film that we saw there detailed the life of the Spanish explorer Hernando de Soto. On April 6, 1538, having already conquered Peru, de Soto and his fleet sailed from Spain, via Cuba. In May, 1539, they eventually reached Tampa Bay in Florida. For the next three years, de Soto and his conquistadors explored the south east of the US, facing attacks from the natives and enslaving many of them as they progressed. First, they conquered Florida, then Georgia and Alabama, before heading west and discovering the mouth of the Mississippi River as they travelled. This was the first time that European explorers had navigated the Mississippi, but de Soto fell into a fever and died on May 21, 1542, his body being consigned to the river he had discovered. He had lost almost half his men to disease and attacks, but his successor Luis de Moscoso continued the expedition, eventually abandoning it in favour of moving on to Mexico. It's a gripping and informative film.

On the way from the Visitor Centre to the house where we would stay, we tried to find somewhere to have coffee. You'd think in a country like America that would be easy, as it's crammed with Starbucks outlets on every corner, but we could not find anywhere at all. While trawling around half-built shopping malls, we found ourselves in an extraordinary store, along the lines of TK Maxx, called Bargain Hunt, crammed with completely random but very cheap items. This turned out to be the first of many experiences during the holiday of searching for baby clothes for our new granddaughter. This was not something that I had ever dreamt I would do, and I certainly would never have imagined enjoying it, but in fact we found loads of delightful garments that were so cheap they almost paid us to take them away. Nowadays, when we see her wearing them, it always brings back happy memories.

The Sat Nav took us through a golf course and then onto the forecourt of quite a substantial property. What would these strangers be like? How would we get on? These were the questions that were preoccupying us and I'm certain were also troubling Tim and Marnie, the parents of our friend, as they awaited our arrival. We were complete strangers, thrown together by a quirk of fate and the whole experience could have been embarrassing and difficult. As it turned out, it was a delight. We liked them a lot and we're pretty sure they liked us too.

Like many Americans we were meeting along the road, one of their first priorities was to make clear to us that they were liberal, open-minded and anti-Trump. This immediately established a good rapport and the evening was spent in the way that people meeting each other for the first time tend to behave. We told each other about our lives and compared notes on life experiences. Tim had got in some ale for me, so that was an excellent start, but with my awful choosiness about food, I was slightly anxious about what might be offered to us. In fact, Marnie had obviously spent a long time creating a pot of gumbo, a delicious southern speciality. Tim, meanwhile, was keen to know what plans we had and how he could help to make everything run smoothly. As we were tired, an earlyish night was sensible and we were suitably humbled as they showed us to our accommodation, which was effectively a luxury suite, our own section of the house with a huge four-poster bed and an en-suite bathroom.

In the morning, they took us on a carefully planned tour of Tupelo. For some reason, I had thought it might be a bit of a dump, but, on the contrary, Tupelo turned out to be an extremely pleasant town with wide, open streets and plenty of parks and greenery. We were taken round the suburban streets, skirted the area of Elvis's birthplace, drove past the store where Elvis bought his first guitar and had a preview of the Lyric Theatre, where we would go the next night.

In the centre, we visited a delightfully quaint old-school bookstore called Reed's Gum Tree. Our new friends knew all the staff and we were immediately greeted with great joy by everyone there. We arrived at the tail-end of a book presentation by a new author. For some reason, both Birgit and I wrongly thought that we knew of her and had read an article about her book. It was her autobiography, and told of a difficult upbringing and suffering at the hands an abusive husband, before a final triumphant rise to fame as an author. It seemed rude not to purchase a book, but it turned out to be an extremely slim volume, certainly not the one we thought it was, and definitely not a great work of literature. My purchase of a rock and roll kids' book for granddaughter Ella was a lot more successful.

Eventually, we set off on our own to explore and the first port of call was, of course, Elvis's birthplace. Elvis (full name Elvis Aaron Presley) was born in Tupelo, on January 8, 1935. His parents were Vernon and Gladys Presley and Elvis was born in a two-room house largely built by hand by his father. Elvis was one of twin brothers but his brother, Jesse Garon, was stillborn and Elvis remained the only child. Elvis grew up in Tupelo surrounded by his extended family, including his grandparents, aunts, uncles and cousins.

Located just off Old Sautillo Road on the edge of Tupelo, the house had no electricity or indoor plumbing.

Nashville Skyline

Home Of The Biscuits

Swampers' HQ

Dyess Colony

Crossroads

Elvis's Birthplace

Hmmm …

Cheers, Loretta

In the mid-1930s, East Tupelo was an area inhabited mainly by poor sharecroppers and factory workers, but even they earned more than the Presleys, who were forced to rely on welfare. Financially, times were consistently hard for Vernon and Gladys and they had to move out of the house where Elvis was born when he was only a few years old. The couple had various jobs while in Tupelo and moved house several times during the thirteen years they lived in Mississippi. From 1938 to 1939, Vernon was in prison, having been convicted of forgery (he had altered a cheque). Indeed, all his life he seems to have been involved in petty crime and found it difficult to sustain employment. The birthplace museum admirably refuses to brush over this difficult aspect of the Presley family life, and the whole thing felt more refreshingly honest than the deification we were later to encounter at Graceland.

It was ragingly hot, over 100 degrees, as we sought sanctuary and coolness in the reconstructed local church where Elvis had first started to sing. It was here that he first came across the gospel music which was so influential on his career. In the church, a film presentation creates the atmosphere of a service and gives more of an insight into small town life for the young family. The church has been moved from its original site and rebuilt near the tiny house where Elvis was born and spent his first years. It was known as a "shotgun cabin" because it was possible to shoot a bullet through the front and out the back without hitting anything. Effectively, they all lived in one room and slept in one bedroom but it was a quite extraordinary feeling to be in the actual house where he grew up. The security is extremely light-touch, with just one elderly lady welcoming you into the house. Of course, there is an enormous souvenir shop selling all kinds of tat, but in the main it is a very understated museum, which does its job admirably. Afterwards, we wandered through the sweltering grounds and round the Lake Of Reflection that has been built nearby.

As we strolled up Tupelo's main street, we were approached by a friendly family who enquired if they could help us in any way. This was a delightfully welcoming gesture, and when we replied that we were actually fine, they gave us their card and said we could call them at any time. This seemed to be another example of Southern hospitality and certainly made us feel right at home. We took a closer look at Tupelo Hardware, seemingly hardly changed since Elvis was bought his first guitar. He was aged 11 when he came in with his mother. The intention was for her to buy him a bicycle but he demanded a rifle. Eventually, they compromised and agreed on the acoustic guitar.

We vaguely followed the Elvis trail and looked in vain for a café that had been recommended to us. I got into trouble for insisting that we spend nearly an hour searching for it. Back in the main street, something was happening. For a start, there were gigantic three-wheeled motorbikes, cowboys on horses and parades of youngsters doing cheerleader-like activities. A few enquiries elicited the information that there was a community festival taking place that day and sure enough, we found a large park with lots of tented food stalls, as well as games such as cornhole, where you throw bags of corn at a board in an attempt to get them into holes. It was impossible not to notice that there was clearly some involuntary segregation going on here, as we were virtually the only white faces in the large crowds. The atmosphere was extremely friendly, and it seemed strange that there was so little intermingling of the races.

The big problem was that a sudden and unexpected storm brought an end to the heatwave and pretty much ruined the entire event. We felt terribly sorry for the organizers, as everybody ran for what little shelter there was and huddled under the rapidly collapsing tents. In the spirit of The Show Must Go On, the music on the stage continued regardless, with absolutely nobody anywhere near the performers or paying any attention. At one stage, a hapless rapper was barking his no doubt incendiary lyrics while three stagehands desperately tried to sweep away the torrents of water around him with completely inadequate squeegees. It was a miracle that no one was electrocuted. Most of the speeches from the likes of the Mayor and the Chairman of the Chamber of Commerce were semi-inaudible but nonetheless it was possible to catch a very positive message in each of them: inclusivity and harmony. We had a beer, ate some fries and felt generally great.

Our hosts had done something very kind. They had realised that, on the very day we were visiting, there was an Elvis tribute show taking place in the beautiful old historic Lyric Theatre in Tupelo. I am certainly not a fan of tribute shows but I figured that an Elvis tribute actually happening in Tupelo would have to be pretty good, and indeed, that is how it turned out. Rejoicing in the name Cody Slaughter, this was one of the South's premier Elvis acts and they had bought us, at some expense, tickets for the sold-out show. What's more, they had invited some of their oldest and best friends over in order to meet us for aperitifs. We were pleased to meet Brad and Louise. Brad was a very accomplished photographer and brought over examples of some of his photos of life in the Mississippi Delta. His wife Louise had been brought up in the Delta and had many tales to tell. No tale was better than Brad's story of his grandfather, and we basked in the feeling of being given exclusive access to history as he told it.

In 1903, Brad's great grandfather had founded a wholesale grocery business in Tupelo that survived under family ownership until 1975. His grandfather, Roy, was the second-generation owner and a generous soul. It's well known that Vernon Presley spent some time in jail when Elvis was young. Elvis and his mother Gladys remained in Tupelo while Vernon was "away." When Vernon returned, it was almost impossible for him to get employment because of his record, but Brad's grandfather, Roy, was the only one who would give Vernon a job. Vernon worked hard and over a three-year period became a delivery truck driver. However, Vernon came up short on deliveries several times and it was rumoured that he was confiscating goods for his own use. After several such incidents, Roy eventually felt that he had to let Vernon go. It was this that led directly to Vernon, Gladys, and Elvis having to leave Tupelo and move to Memphis. The rest, as they say, is history.

So off we all went to the Lyric Theatre, which was largely packed with octogenarians. Certain aspects of the evening were ill-judged, for example, having a dire generic Country singer as a support and allowing him to go on too long, then Cody doing two long sets himself, one focusing on the 50s, the other on the 60s. The main crime in my mind was using backing tracks, but nonetheless it was a really enjoyable evening. Cody himself came originally from Arkansas and won the accolade of "Ultimate Elvis Tribute Artist" in Memphis in 2011. His moves were accurate, if slightly studied, and the hip twisting and pelvis thrusting became a wee bit repetitive, but just to be in Tupelo listening to Elvis songs felt like a quite magical privilege.

Much of the chat in the interval focused on the compère, a "Smashy and Nicey"-style obsequious presenter with very obviously dyed black hair. This was Jack Curtis, himself another Elvis impersonator of slightly less fame. Jack's brother, Kevin, yet another Elvis tribute artist, we were told, had recently been implicated by a fourth Elvis tribute artist in some attempted ricin attacks. Packages had been sent through the mail to several major political figures, including President Obama, a senator and a Mississippi judge. For whatever reason, it appears that one Elvis was jealous of, or angry at, the other Elvis and sought to frame him, resulting in a visit from the local FBI and Kevin Curtis's consequent short spell behind bars during the investigation. Eventually, Kevin was released and the police arrested Everett Dutschke, a martial arts instructor, with whom Kevin had been having a vicious long-term feud.

Another weird circumstance in all this was that Kevin had apparently lost his job at the local medical centre after accusing it of storing huge numbers of body parts and organs. Naturally, such a deliciously lurid small-town scandal was music to my ears.

We knew that the next day would take us into the Delta and that the theme would change to blues. Tim had been brought up in Oxford, Mississippi and was exceptionally knowledgeable about the Delta region. It was from his mother's childhood stories of growing up there that he had formed his interest in the region and its history. Every few minutes, he would disappear into his office and come out with various maps and downloads that he had kindly created for us.

In order to move on, the first thing to do was agree on a route. I had become fixated on visiting the BB King Museum, but hadn't realised that it would involve a major detour. The museum itself is in Indianola, but we had already booked to stay the next night in Clarksdale. Tim described to us the endless flatness of the Delta area, almost all of it reclaimed from swampland and now devoted to cotton and rice growing and a surprisingly large number of penitentiaries. This was where the blues had been born, and I was determined to find out more about it. Tim spoke very movingly about the area and his feelings for it, so much so that I invited him to write down his thoughts:

"It is practically indescribable. I can offer the title of James Cobb's book - that it is 'The Most Southern Place On Earth.' It surely is. Or David L. Cohn's description: 'The Mississippi Delta begins in the lobby of the Peabody Hotel in Memphis and ends on Catfish Row in Vicksburg.' Or I could borrow Cohn's phrase about Natchez, MS, opining it a place 'in this world but not of this world.' The outsider's pre-visit impression is often binary when it comes to cultures in the Delta: white planter and African-American slave/labourer. Of course, the reality is much more diverse. As the U.S. Park Service describes the entire Lower Mississippi Delta region: 'The Delta's cultural traditions are as rich and diverse as its natural resources ... Over the centuries, American Indians, French, Arab, Spanish, African German, English, Irish, Scots-Irish, Jewish, Italian, Chinese, Mexican (and more recently, Southeast Asian) peoples have established themselves and maintained their identities.' On top of all that, and in summary, the Delta is indeed an eccentric, often weird place."

This diversity is indeed not what most outsiders would immediately associate with the Mississippi Delta, with its history of slavery and its still persisting racial tensions.

CROSSROADS

Tim was right about the endless flat roads but had given us some tips about scenic side routes, and eventually, after a good chunk more of the Natchez Trace, we arrived in Indianola, an unassuming village where the astonishingly modern and high-tech B.B. King museum is to be found. The museum, which opened in 2008, has the stated mission to "empower, unite and heal through music, art and education and share with the world the rich cultural heritage of the Mississippi Delta".

It exists in memory of Riley B. King, whose life in the Mississippi Delta started with a difficult and challenging youth. His parents split when he was four and when his mother died (when he was nine), he moved in with his grandmother. After she died, Riley moved from Indianola to Kilmichael, Mississippi, where he was taken in by the Cartledges, a white family who had a small farm, where he was able to live and work. Wayne Cartledge bought Riley his first guitar and encouraged him to judge people by actions rather than skin colour.

As his guitar playing improved, Riley thought about relocating to Memphis, but he had recently married. The decision to move was finally taken when he had an accident and damaged a tractor. Scared that he might get into trouble with his employer, he took his guitar and headed to Memphis. After spending a year hanging out with his cousin Bukka White, Riley returned to the farm and paid off his debt, before finally moving to Memphis for good.

For over ten years, Riley (now known as B.B. King) and his band toured the "Chitlin' Circuit", which was an informal network of African-American blues clubs in the South-East of the US. He also presented a radio show and did much recording. His first hit on the Billboard charts was "Three O'Clock Blues", in 1951.

B.B. developed an unusual style of blues, featuring a big band style coupled with electric lead guitar. Just as the blues was beginning to go out of fashion, along came the British blues boom and Riley's music was discovered by a whole new audience. Bands like the Rolling Stones, Led Zeppelin and Cream had grown up listening to and emulating B.B. and other black American blues performers.

For the rest of his life, B.B. King was a major international star, touring incessantly with a large entourage, always treating all his associates generously and courteously. Above all, he was an incredibly hard worker, as well as a fine musician and singer. He won several Grammys and also found time to have fifteen children, whom he seldom saw, as he was always away touring.

Despite the slightly jarring contrast between the conditions of poverty of the blues musicians and the brand new and extremely expensively kitted-out museum, it's an informative and enjoyable experience, complete with video walls and enough exhibits to keep you occupied for several hours. These include, of course, B.B.'s favourite guitar Lucille. There were fifteen Lucilles in all, all of them literally "played to death". The museum isn't only a homage to King, but also explains the wider blues history and culture. Each year, there is a B.B. King Homecoming Festival but as he, of course, can no longer come home (having died in Las Vegas in 2015 at the age of 89), it is now a mini blues festival.

As there was torrential rain outside, we spent half an hour in the gift shop. This gave me my usual opportunity to snort at the outrageous prices, announce that I would never buy anything in a place like this, and then leave with a bag containing a t-shirt, a mug and a fridge magnet. Basically, in a situation like that, you know you're never going to be back, so you have to grab some kind of souvenir, despite its disgracefully high price. Apart from the museum, we didn't find much to do in Indianola and so, having examined B.B.'s tour bus, still parked outside the museum, we continued across the Delta towards Clarksdale.

The cotton fields were endless, only dotted with the occasional tumbledown shack and ancient cotton gins, water towers and grain stores. The poverty of the area was plain to see, but the atmosphere was exactly what you would anticipate when researching the history of the blues.

As the flat road reached the outskirts of Clarksdale, on the left we could see what looked like a large derelict farm, fronted by something called the Hopson Commissary. We later learnt this was a name for a general store, but the Sat Nav was telling us that this was where we were to spend the night. We'd been recommended the Shackup Inn by a dear English friend of mine, so we vaguely knew what to expect. The Shackup is based around an old cotton gin and the accommodation is in former sharecroppers' shacks which have been updated. Its slogan is "The Ritz We Ain't", which is accurate enough.

The Delta plantation system had begun in the 19th century, when white farmers went to Mississippi in order to create fertile farmland. They had to clear the forests and hold back the Mississippi River with levees, all of which work was carried out by slaves. Eventually, as a result of the slaves' labour, the Delta became the richest cotton-farming area in the US. Mississippi was one of the most repressive states for black slaves, with a reputation for extreme levels of violence. Eventually, slavery was replaced by the sharecropping system, but life for the workers was little better. Under the system, sharecroppers rented the land and paid for it with a percentage of the crop. As it was virtually impossible to make any kind of profit, it was a hard and unrewarding life, that eventually came to an end when mechanisation was introduced and most of the workers were no longer needed. Reading about this made me feel ambivalent, to say the least, about staying in a hotel that had possibly once housed slave workers.

We found somewhere to park at the back of the collection of shacks and the first thing that happened was that within thirty seconds of stepping out of the car, I had been bitten half to death by vicious mosquitoes. The humid weather means that these bastards thrive in this area. With difficulty, we dragged the wheeled suitcases across a soggy lawn and into the back door of the Inn. At reception, contrary to expectations, we found someone who showed very little interest in us and wasn't even vaguely friendly. She informed us straight away that the bar was closed, that there were no other drinks available and the breakfast consisted of help-yourself cereals and muffins. Well, there's a surprise. Although this was the staple breakfast provided in all the motels, we had had some hope that this quirky place might be a little different.

The room we had booked turned out to be part of a converted grain store, and was, as my friend had promised, a lot more luxurious than the external environment would have led you to believe. To get there, you had to ascend some creaky stairs, where it was noticeable that everything was covered in dust and dirt. This was, of course, part of the ambience, but it also made you feel that it gave them a good excuse to cut down on cleaning staff. In the room, for some reason, a James Bond clip was running on repeat on the TV screen. I meant to ask why this was but forgot. Instead, we lay down to rest and use Paul's kettle to make a cup of tea with the PG tips that we had brought with us. All in all, it was a shame, because the Inn contains a super cool venue with a stage and PA, but it was deserted. I'd still recommend a visit, but we had caught the Shackup on an "off" day.

The unhelpful lady in reception was no more forthcoming about what there might be to do in the evening, other than to tell us quite clearly that there was no live music available because it was a Sunday. This seemed hard to believe, in view of Clarksdale's reputation as a live music mecca. That was indeed the reason we had decided to visit the town at all.

Clarksdale was founded by John Clark in 1848. It's situated at the head the Sunflower River and, in true blues tradition, is bisected by a railroad line. Frequent floods, a fire in 1889 and poor roads all impeded the early growth of Clarksdale, but since 1900 it has grown consistently, and it is now one of the largest cities in the Mississippi Delta. The first cotton crop commercially produced entirely by machinery, from planting to baling, was grown in 1944 by the Hopson Planting Company in Clarksdale. Nowadays, the city trades unashamedly and rightly on its history as "Home Of The Blues". Sam Cooke, the "King of Soul", was born in Clarksdale, as were John Lee Hooker, Ike Turner and

Eddie Boyd. Muddy Waters grew up in Clarksdale and Bessie Smith died there in 1937. In the Riverside Hotel in Clarksdale, her room is preserved as it was back then and is never rented out. W.C. Handy, the playwright Tennessee Williams and the Staple Singers have all lived in Clarksdale.

Before leaving the Shackup Inn for the evening, we studied the guidebook and found a place called Levon's, which claimed to have regular live music, so we headed there. This also was a slight disappointment because it was a modern and rather expensive eaterie, recently opened by an Australian restauranteur. The only music available was a corpulent young white bluesman playing an electric guitar very badly and loudly enough to make any conversation during the pretty average meal completely impossible. Let's hope the venue wasn't named after Levon Helm, because the Big Pink veteran would have turned in his grave. There was nothing for it but to have an early night.

The next day was dedicated to exploring Clarksdale, and what non-stop fun it turned out to be. As we pulled up at a traffic-light junction just outside of the centre,

Birgit spotted the Crossroads monument on the corner. This was the intersection of Routes 61 and 49. Risking life and limb, I leapt out of the car to take a photograph of the famous crossed guitars, symbolising where rivals claimed that Delta blues legend Robert Johnson had sold his soul to the Devil in return for guitar virtuosity.

Having spurned the Shackup Inn's breakfast offer, we headed to Grandma's Pancakes for the most delicious breakfast of the entire trip. Galumphing pancakes with maple syrup, bacon and eggs made us feel very American.

It was already clear that central Clarksdale was full of small, independent local businesses and almost entirely free of chains. First up was the tourist information office, housed in the old train station. As we entered, we spotted a small, elderly man in dungarees and were introduced to him and his friend, with whom he was chatting. This turned out to be a very exciting encounter, because the gentleman in question revealed himself as Vic Barbieri, the very craftsman who had designed and built the famous Crossroads symbol. He said he'd just spent the morning restringing the guitars with aircraft wire and told us all about the regular maintenance he has to do on the monument, so that it meets the expectations of the passing blues tourists. Vic was an absolute gentleman and it felt quite a privilege to meet such an important person in the town. He gave me his autograph and also confirmed that, as far as he was concerned, THAT crossroads is THE crossroads.

Among bluesologists, debate rages about which particular crossroads was the one in question. Many claim that the Crossroads was in Rosedale, Mississippi rather than Clarksdale, but, along with Vic, I beg to differ. The lyrics from Johnson's song Crossroads (much covered by UK bands, notably Cream) say:

I went down to the crossroads, tried to flag a ride

Down to the crossroads, tried to flag a ride

Nobody seemed to know me, everybody passed me by

And I'm going down to Rosedale, take my rider by my side

Going down to Rosedale, take my rider by my side

You can still barrel house, baby, on the riverside.

If he was "going down to Rosedale", he couldn't have been in Rosedale, could he? Well, I agree it's hardly conclusive, but as the Devil doesn't exist, it's largely academic, because he couldn't have sold his soul to him anyway. Adding to the mythology was Johnson's death at the age of 27, variously described as having been either from strychnine poisoning or syphilis.

Set out on the traditional American grid system, Clarksdale is very easy to navigate. First, we visited a souvenir and book shop, whose owner told us more about the Shackup. More and more small properties were being added to the field, he explained, and people were buying them individually to rent out to tourists. Indeed, the bookshop owner himself had just bought one and was in the process of doing it up. In the shop, we encountered a Dutch couple who were on a similar odyssey to us. The gentleman claimed to be an "Americana" music journalist on a research trip, but googling him produced no results.

Whenever we are on holiday, we tend to bump into the same people again and again. One time, on the island of Grenada, there was a couple whom we christened the Blue Caps, because they both had identical, guess what, blue caps. They were, however, extremely unfriendly and merely looked away each time we said, "Wow, hello again, what a coincidence!" The Dutch couple were completely different and engaged in animated conversation each of the four times we bumped into them.

Minutes later, we were in a T-shirt printing establishment where you could select what pattern you wanted and choose different wording. This was the opposite of the B.B. King souvenir shop experience, as the poor guy can barely have been making any profit at all, so cheap were his wares. His profits will have dived even more that day, because he repeatedly messed up the printing system and had to throw away a total of four T-shirts. I, of course, emerged with two T-shirts, a cap emblazoned with the Crossroads symbol and another fridge magnet, while our Dutch friends bought similar amounts of merch. Well, you only live once.

We spent nearly two hours in the official Delta Blues Museum next to the tourist office. It was becoming slightly spooky to find the Dutch couple round every corner we turned and by now I was getting slightly fed up with his boasting about his journalistic achievements. The Delta Blues Museum, however, was just wonderful.

Established as a stand-alone museum in 1999, it's the state's oldest music museum. It's housed in the historic Clarksdale freight depot, built in 1918 for the Yazoo and Mississippi Valley Railroad, having originally been located in a school and subsequently in a library. The museum is big, occupying the former freight area, and has an extension focusing on Muddy Waters and containing a reconstruction of the cabin where he lived.

ZZ Top helped to raise funds for the original museum. Guitarist Billy Gibbons arranged for some "Muddywood" guitars to be built from boards used in Muddy Waters' cabin. There is one of these guitars on permanent display in the museum, which we studied with alacrity. Indeed, I took a photo of it, despite the many threatening notices forbidding photography. I have never understood why you aren't allowed to take photos in museums. It took a couple of hours to examine all the displays, featuring the likes of Son House, B.B. King, Charlie Musselwhite, Mississippi Fred McDowell, Big Mama Thornton and Bo Diddley. Once again, I felt tears welling up as we rounded each corner to find further displays of guitars, stage gear, original lyrics and acetates.

There is (or was) another museum in Clarksdale, and it has to be one of the strangest in the world. A Dutch gentleman called Theo Dasbach had been collecting rock and pop memorabilia for decades and initially, having given up a career in international banking, opened his museum in the nineties in the Netherlands, before taking the plunge and bringing the whole lot over to Clarksdale in 2005, establishing it as a non-profit attraction. Basically, it's a delightfully chaotic mishmash of one person's music memorabilia and has little to do with its blues location. I was fascinated to see various sixties Dutch and German 45 rpm singles that I actually own myself, but, along with the likes of Robert Plant and Keith Richards, Theo was irresistibly attracted to the blues and increased that element of the collection. Among many other gems are highly valuable rare test pressings by a young Robert Johnson, including "Love in Vain" - later covered by the Stones.

When we visited, it was apparent from a small notice that the museum was up for sale, and, on the face of it, at a bargain price of $195,000, including a built-in apartment. However, it was hard to see how it could be a viable business and the look on Birgit's face when I suggested we should sell up and move to Clarksdale told me all I needed to know. Now the exhibits are being sold off one by one, in order to finance Theo's well-earned retirement.

I don't know why, but I felt a zen-like feeling of happiness the whole day. I suppose this was because, when I first started listening to blues as a student in the late sixties, I would never have dreamt in a million years that I would one day have the opportunity to visit its fulcrum. On every corner were signs commemorating local musicians, and dotted around were authentic-seeming Juke Joints and scruffy bars with posters advertising live music every night. Yes, we had indeed been misinformed by the grumpy receptionist and in fact there had apparently been in a sensational gig the night before at an iconic bar called Reds, which annoyingly had been attended by our Dutch stalkers.

We obviously had to enter one of these establishments, and chose Ground Zero, because we knew it was co-owned by local resident and ambassador for the area, Morgan Freeman. This was indeed an impressive building if you were looking for an authentic blues vibe, dilapidated from outside and scruffy and filthy inside, just what you want. The pool table looked as if it had been hit by a bomb. Even though it was lunch time, we decided a beer was appropriate and it was disappointing that the beer was, in fact, "off" and undrinkable. As we were the only customers, it wasn't a particularly exciting experience and we soon moved on. Later on, someone told me that it was actually a relatively new building and all the scruffiness was in fact cleverly- designed "shabby chic", created to give tourists a false feeling of authenticity.

It was time to check into our airbnb, which we had found on the internet. It was an impressive, Colonial-style white edifice called the Bohemian White House, where we were greeted by a delightful ex-model called Magical Madge, who owns the bnb with her husband and blues tour guide Chilly Billy. I was in such a good mood that I didn't even mind petting their little dog Dandy, even though, on the face of it, I can't stand dogs. We repaired to our extremely luxurious room and I immediately plunged into the huge freestanding bath, which I filled with the free potions provided.

Madge and Billy do regular house concerts in their huge front room, replete with a grand piano, and their offering put other airbnbs firmly in the shade. You were welcome to help yourself to anything from the fridge, which was fully stocked with tasty and organic items, a very long way from the average US hotel breakfast.

Madge was a lot more informative about live music than the previous night's person had been, even though she also, annoyingly, had attended the brilliant blues jam the night before at Reds and said we should have been there. She knew about a Monday night open mic back at the Hopson Commissary, so we headed there in the early evening. It turned out that the barman who was in charge of booking the acts had not got round to doing so, and therefore was performing himself. For two hours, we sat open-mouthed over our bottles of Dos Equis as he performed a set of extraordinary cover versions, such as you are never likely to hear from your average singer-songwriter troubadour. There was no hint of any blues, as he brought his first set to a raging climax consisting of the Who's "Squeeze Box" and "The End" by The

Doors. The assembled chain-smoking rednecks (mainly there for the free gumbo dispensed by the owner on Mondays) were not impressed, but I was so much in awe that I started quizzing him about the establishment. It emerged that, despite being on the same piece of land and indeed pretty much physically attached to each other, the Shackup and Hopson's are deadly rivals who have no contact and compete for customers with virtually identical music venues.

Tossing a few dollars into his bucket (nobody else did) we headed off to the Bluesberry Café, where Madge had told us there was to be a harmonica battle. The café was a tiny shop with a rickety stage near the door and a huddle of extremely dodgy looking characters in the porch. Despite the lovely surroundings of the White House, and its proximity to Downtown, Madge had made it quite clear to us that we should on no account consider walking into town on our own.

Inside the café, I tried to order food at the crowded bar from a lady whose system seemed entirely chaotic. She looked and acted as if she were sky high on drugs, with an extraordinary system of pieces of paper with orders on them which seemed unlikely ever to be fulfilled. As I waited, I was engaged in slightly daunting conversation by two separate young gentlemen who were clearly on crystal meth or something similar. You sensed that it was important not to say the wrong thing to them, as I ordered two pasta dishes and we sat down to watch the entertainment.

On stage was a house band and various harmonica players who would get up and join them, sometimes on their own and sometimes in groups. Interestingly, all were white. They would proceed to blueswail at each other in a highly impressive but somewhat repetitive manner. They all had those strange gun belts round their waists, in which they kept their harmonicas, plus small attaché cases with extra ammunition in different keys. It ended in dramatic fashion with one of the players flat out and seemingly unconscious on the stage, while the other clearly was experiencing a panic attack on account of not finding the right key of harmonica at the right moment. After about an hour, the pasta finally arrived and by a miracle was absolutely delicious. God knows how the chef had understood what we wanted.

LONG DISTANCE INFORMATION

Well, Elvis moved from Tupelo to Memphis, B.B. King moved from Indianola to Memphis and the guy with the museum in Clarksdale commutes from Memphis on a daily basis, so it was finally time for us to head to the city that features in so many songs. There's Chuck Berry's "Memphis Tennessee", Johnny Cash's "I'm Going To Memphis" and my favourite, a touching lament by Austin Lucas called "Alone In Memphis". It was only a matter of seventy-five miles before we hit Elvis Presley Boulevard and inevitably turned left instead of right.

Elvis bought Graceland in 1957 when he was only

22, for him to live in with his parents and grandmother. The privacy of the colonial-style property was necessary because of his already huge fame; the previous property he had bought in East Memphis was a magnet for fans. He lived at Graceland for twenty years, during which a number of girlfriends and one wife (Priscilla) were also present, along with the entourage necessary to sustain his career. Elvis eventually died in the master bathroom in 1977, and the property now belongs to his daughter Lisa Marie. It's the second most-visited house in the US after the White House.

When we finally located the car park for Graceland, I was already beginning to get in a bad mood. The lady at the entrance was plain rude, it was hard to find a parking slot and the first glimpse of the complex was very similar to the first glimpse of Disneyland: crass and concrete. The next shock was the entry price. We went for the cheapest option, which was a tour of the house and admission to Elvis's aeroplanes. This cost us 41 dollars each. If we'd been real fans and wanted to see his costumes and his cars, it would have cost us 61 dollars. And as for the various VIP packages … they included one for 2562 dollars which included a one-to-one with Elvis's ghost. Or maybe I imagined that one.

Already, the contrast with the Birthplace, which is run by locals as a charity, was marked. All around us were crap rip-off restaurants selling things such as - surely this is morbid - peanut butter and banana sandwiches. We climbed aboard a minibus, which took us over the busy road from the tourist complex to the actual house. It was a journey of two minutes. God forbid that anybody should have considered the possibility of walking.

The first impression of the house was the same as anybody who has been to Graceland will tell you: it's small. I don't mean small by the standards of your house or my house, but it's not really what you expect a rock star mansion to be like. Despite the presence of a Jungle Room (later used as a recording studio), a Billiards Room and a TV Room, everything feels quite small in scale. It's surprisingly unpretentious. I kept saying, "Well, if I was a millionaire musician, I think I'd buy a place like this". Twenty-two rooms and eight bathrooms would probably be sufficient. We shuffled through the crowds with a device like an iPad round our necks, which, for me at least, stubbornly refused to work. Luckily the tour wasn't long, mainly because you're only allowed to see very small parts of the house (you can't go upstairs at all, for example). The noticeable thing was an almost religious feeling throughout and the worshipful atmosphere. For me the most memorable bits were the Raquetball Room where Elvis was active on the morning of his death, and the paddocks outside, where he kept his horses.

Before leaving, you are permitted to spend a period of reflection in the Meditation Garden, by the graves of Elvis, his parents Vernon and Gladys and his grandmother Minnie Mae. Alongside is also a memorial for Elvis's twin Jesse Garon. Elvis's funeral was held on August 18, 1977. A reported 75,000 people flocked to Memphis to pay their respects to him, the line of mourners stretching for miles along Elvis Presley Boulevard. After his funeral, his body was initially buried in Forest Hills Cemetery in Memphis. His mother's body was moved from her original grave to lie alongside Elvis there, but before long, the graves began to be tampered with and were transferred to Graceland.

Back over the road, we were allowed to ascend the

steps to his two private jets, one large one called Lisa Marie, after his daughter, and a smaller one called Hound Dog II. I have to admit that these gave me a bigger buzz than the house, but only because it allowed me to imagine what it must have been like to be a member of Led Zeppelin.

Now it was time to find the air bnb we had booked. We had very high hopes for this place, because it had been recommended by a friend. I reckon that, if we had been there a few months before, it would have been a delight, but as it was, there was a very downbeat atmosphere. The place was called the Memphis Music Mansion and it was, indeed, a huge palatial property with a ground floor the size of a medium-sized concert hall. It, too, had a grand piano right in the centre, but apart from that, it was pretty much empty. Outside was an algae-covered dark brown soup-filled swimming pool, which meant that the anticipated dip was out of the question. The place itself was out in a suburb and next to a busy highway, which crushed our hopes of any public transport or being able to walk into the centre. The main problem was that it was on the point of closure; in fact it was immediately revealed that we were the last guests.

The place was run by a couple who had set it up a few years previously with the innovative idea of running an air bnb that also offered house concerts. This was the concept explained on the website and we had high hopes of musical entertainment. It was clear that these hopes would also remain unfulfilled, because, as they were about to leave the house in the next couple of days, all the furniture had been removed and a ghostly, deserted atmosphere reigned. By stark contrast with the White House in Clarksdale, the fridge was completely empty and we were offered nothing at all in the way of sustenance or potential for making ourselves breakfast.

The room itself was serviceable, if creaky, and did at least contain one of the features advertised, in the form of a record player and a box of vinyl albums. The other frustrating thing was the hosts' inability to offer us any brochures, maps or anything that would have been useful to us. We more or less forced them to at least give us a couple of tips as to where we could go, but clearly and understandably, their minds were concentrated on their task of packing up and leaving.

Bizarrely, the only item on the ground floor, apart from the piano, was a lonely suitcase. This belonged to the Australian singer-songwriter Emily Barker (yes, the one I was going to speak to in Nashville but didn't), a recent guest who had somehow succeeded in leaving it behind when returning to the UK. On top of her other woes, our hostess was trying to deal with courier companies and get it picked up.

After they had come to terms with the fact that we actually wanted to walk somewhere, they did tell us how to get to a local area where there were restaurants and bars. The live music offering was a terrible covers band and we were foolishly tempted into going into a chain restaurant with a New Orleans theme. This was an awful experience for three reasons. Firstly, the food was plates full of extremely heavy unidentified sludge, which lay heavily in our stomachs for days. We sat outside on a patio and the second problem was that the two families on the next table were having an ultra right-wing conversation at very high volume, to the extent that we had to move away.

The third thing fills me with shame and increasing worry about my mental state as I enter my seventies. I am forever paranoid about dementia, as my sister suffered from it for many years, to the extent that, for at least the last ten years of her life, she didn't know who any of her family were. So, every time I forget something or lose something, I tell myself, "Oh no, it's started". On this occasion, it really was a stinker.

When the time came to pay the bill, I reached behind me for my jacket, which I was certain was hanging on the back of my chair, only to discover that there was nothing there. An immediate sense of panic came over me, because the jacket contained my mobile phone, my wallet and my passport. For a moment, I assumed that it must still be hanging on the chair of the table we had vacated, but it wasn't. I called the waiter over and asked if he had seen the stray garment. At this stage, I was scrabbling in flowerbeds next to the patio, in case the jacket had somehow fallen into them. Two minutes later, the waiter reappeared, jacket miraculously in hand, but where he had found it really gave me cause to fear for my sanity. As we had entered, we had stopped at the front desk, as you do in American restaurants, to be allocated a table and check over the menu. It appeared that I had simply put my jacket on the table and left it there, where it must have remained for the next ninety minutes or so, in full view of everyone and containing my most valuable possessions.

This is a good moment to talk about the American tipping culture. It is very difficult for Europeans to comprehend, because, in the main, we are used to tipping only if we are very happy with the service we have received. In America, tipping is culturally compulsory and only to be withheld if the service is absolutely appalling. My friend Paul is extremely well-versed in tipping convention, and at the end of any given meal will whip out his calculator and work out precisely how much to add on to the bill. If I suggest giving even a few cents less than he has worked out, he is filled with horror and tells me off in no uncertain terms. After all the years I have been going to America, I have finally come to terms with it, but it still comes as a shock that the bill you pay at the end of the evening bears little resemblance to what you have worked out by looking at the menu.

Anyway, on this occasion, the waiter who had found my jacket was delighted to receive a much higher tip than even he had been expecting.

We had had certain doubts about the prospect of visiting Memphis, because some acquaintances had warned us that it was a very violent and dangerous city, but as usual we wandered round in blissful innocence and at no stage felt even vaguely threatened in the least. One thing we had to do on the way back to the mansion was try to purchase something that we could eat for breakfast. We passed a large store which was an imitation of Whole Foods. It was indeed full of healthy items such as fruit and vegetables, but the prices were astronomical. Maybe this gives a clue as to why so many Americans either eat out or eat junk, which can help to explain some of the obesity problems that are so plain to see. In the end we bought a packet of cereal, some blueberries and a carton of what we thought was milk. The bill for this came to nearly twenty dollars and in the morning, we were horrified to find that the milk was something called "half and half" which consisted of half milk and half cream and also - shudder - was sweetened.

The breakfast experience was less than pleasant and we quickly called an Uber to take us into the city centre. This was the first time I'd demonstrated my new-found Uber skills to Birgit and I could see she was impressed. Funny how, after more than forty years, I can still get a little buzz from impressing a lady.

I'm ashamed to say that I have sometimes watched Michael Portillo's Great Rail Journeys. The magnificence of the trains and the countryside has occasionally allowed me to overlook the fact that he is a badly-dressed Tory prick. Something in the depths of my memory reminded me that he had once visited the Peabody Hotel in Memphis and documented the surreal ceremony of the Duck March. This was something I badly wanted to experience, so we arranged for the driver to drop us off there.

Portillo explained how the Duck March had originated. In the 1930s, Frank Schutt, who was the Peabody's general manager, went to Arkansas for a weekend's hunting with a friend. When they returned to the hotel, a little worse for wear from Tennessee whiskey, they thought it would be a laugh to put some of their live duck decoys (yes, live decoys were legal back then) into the fountain which formed the centrepiece of the Peabody Hotel's ground floor. When the guests came down in the morning, they were all delighted to see the ducks, and so the tradition was born. An animal trainer called Bellman Pembroke later introduced the idea of having the ducks live on the roof, descend daily in the elevator and march to their fountain. Pembroke was then Peabody "Duckmaster" for fifty years, finally retiring in 1991.

One thing we have discovered over years of travelling is that, even if you could not possibly afford to stay there, there is nothing to stop you sauntering into luxury hotels and partaking of any of their facilities that are free. For example, in the Caribbean, you can enter a five-star establishment and use the swimming pools and jacuzzis with impunity. It helps if you buy a cup of coffee, but it's not actually required. The people who enter the Peabody every morning shortly before eleven do so mainly in order to experience the Duck Ceremony, and that's what we did, marching up the sweeping staircase and taking up a drake's eye view from the balcony. After an introductory speech from the liveried Duckmaster, who explained the legend, the lift doors parted to reveal a small posse of waddling ducks, who proceeded to amble down the red carpet and hop into the small fountain in the centre of the lobby.

Now from an animal welfare point of view, I assume it can't be very nice for them to spend the whole day indoors swimming around in a little circle, but who am I to speculate on the psychological condition of a duck? It can't be claimed that it's much of a spectacle, but it's certainly a fun experience. To my shame and humiliation, we then repaired to the gift shop and invested in a couple of overpriced and rubbish souvenirs. However (I hope you see the theme here) they were for our granddaughter, so that was all right. She is a good excuse for any pointless purchases.

Far from the terrifying prospect that had been painted to us in advance, we found Memphis to be a charming and pleasant city, almost Parisian in the amount of greenery and the spacious pedestrianised boulevards. Before long, we had found a helpful tourist office and the gentleman in there pointed us towards the Mississippi for a brief promenade that took us along the river and up some streets which led to the main focus of the day: The world famous Civil Rights Museum.

Following the map faithfully, we rounded a corner at the top of Main Street and looked where the museum was supposed to be, but all we could see was a very large and not particularly attractive motel. It took several minutes and a lot of turning the map upside down and round for the penny to finally drop this was indeed the Lorraine Motel. No longer functioning for its original purpose, it was in fact the Civil Rights Museum, and what we saw in front of us was the very balcony on which Martin Luther King had been gunned down. That in itself was breathtaking and took a little getting used to, but what awaited us in the museum was one of the most moving experiences either of us had ever had. I know people who have visited this museum numerous times and even the four hours we spent there felt like just scratching the surface. When you reach a certain age, yet every day increase and improve your education, it really is - to use that hackneyed expression - life-affirming.

Dr King and his entourage had been due to spend

the night of April 3, 1964 in the Lorraine Motel. The Lorraine was one of the few Memphis motels at the time that was recognised as being welcoming to African-Americans. King was in Memphis because on February 1, 1968, two garbage collectors, Robert Walker and Echol Cole, had been crushed to death in an accident with a faulty garbage truck. The incident highlighted the bad working conditions and low wages of sanitation workers, who called for a strike, prompted by the deaths of their colleagues. The sanitation workers, all of whom were black, went on strike, setting up picket lines and waving placards with declarations such as "I Am A Man."

King, the USA's most famous civil rights activist, had heard about the industrial action and decided to travel to Memphis to bring national attention to it. He was already a prominent national figure, having led the bus boycott in Montgomery, Alabama. This occurred in 1955, after an African-American woman named Rosa Parks was famously arrested for refusing to give up her bus seat to a white man. Over the following ten years, King had become an iconic civil rights figurehead, leading non-violent protests for racial equality. In 1963, he'd made his "I Have A Dream" speech in New York:

"I have a dream that my four little children will one day live in a nation where they will not be judged by the colour of their skin but by the content of their character," King declared. By the time he made his fateful trip to Memphis, he had been awarded the 1965 Nobel Peace Prize.

During the afternoon of April 3, having checked into Room 306, King left the Lorraine to deliver a speech to a crowd at the Mason Temple Church. Many members of the congregation were striking sanitation workers. King and his colleagues were due to have dinner at the home of the Rev. Samuel Billy Kyles, a local minister. At about 6 p.m., King left his motel room.

As he appeared on the balcony, a shot rang out and a bullet hit King in the head. He was immediately taken to St. Joseph's Hospital, where he was pronounced dead. His assassination triggered riots in cities all across the US. President Lyndon B. Johnson designated April 7, 1968, as a national day of mourning. The following day, King's widow Coretta travelled to Memphis, where she led the striking workers in a peaceful march. A week later, the Memphis sanitation strike ended when the city council accepted the workers' demands and improved both their wages and their working conditions.

The man eventually convicted of King's assassination was James Earl Ray, a forty-year-old known criminal. The conviction was based on the discovery of his fingerprint on the murder weapon. It seemed clear that Ray had shot King from the window of a boarding house opposite the Lorraine Motel. Ray initially evaded arrest and somehow made his way to London, England, where he was detained on June 8 and extradited to the United States. In March, 1969, he pleaded guilty in a Memphis courtroom to King's murder and was sentenced to ninety-nine years in prison. He died in 1998 from complications associated with Hepatitis C.

When you reach the actual motel room that King was staying in on that fateful day, the feeling is hard to describe. You're not just looking at history, you are actually in it. Some people have said that letting you get so close to the scene can be viewed as tasteless, but we found it enhanced the experience dramatically.

Of course, you can't actually lie down on his bed, but a piece of plexiglass separates you from where he spent his last moments. What's more, the museum experience continues over the road where are you are able to look across at the balcony from the actual place where the shots were fired. This museum extension is particularly dramatic and engaging, because it contains a very detailed timeline of the events leading up to the assassination, plus an analysis of the various conspiracy theories. At the end, you realise that it's not even a hundred percent certain that James Earl Ray was the actual assassin.

Different rooms in the museum are dedicated to different aspects of the struggle for civil rights in America. The most shocking of these is the area that gives an insight into the Jim Crow laws. These laws effectively created a racial caste system in the Southern states. In the early part of the twentieth century, black and white people weren't allowed to go to the same schools, share public transport or eat in the same restaurants. Black people were banned from parks, swimming pools, beaches and hospitals. Two events brilliantly reconstructed in the museum are the boycott of segregated buses in Montgomery, Alabama in 1956, and the sit-in in a whites-only diner in Greensboro, North Carolina in 1960. These events kick-started the Civil Rights Movement, as blacks and whites joined together to promote Equal Rights.

All this, and much more, is graphically illustrated in the museum, which features scores of films, interactive displays and enough historical information and interpretation to keep any visitor gripped for hours. Feeling quite breathless, we felt it was time for a little light relief. Most gentlemen of a certain age find anything that moves on rails irresistible, so the dinky little yellow streetcars which ply Main Street were probably more attractive to me than to Birgit, but, as she was in search of a cup of coffee, I unconvincingly assured her that a ride on the streetcar was bound to take us to a coffee house.

It wasn't immediately apparent how much it would cost or how we would pay, but as we mounted, the driver informed us it was a dollar a ride, and that we could stay on board as long as he wanted. As we only had a hundred dollar bill and he had no change, he kindly said, "Don't worry, you can ride for free." This we duly did, all the way to the other end of Main Street, where the terminus is near the gigantic Pyramid entertainment complex, and then all the way back to a faceless and extremely expensive branch of Starbucks, so we both got what we wanted. Nearby was an "artisan" pizzeria and, as we were both heartily fed up with anything that came with fries, a huge pizza was a pleasant prelude to what we assumed would be quite a wild evening on Beale Street.

Music and Memphis are inseparable. Beale Street is now known principally for its blues clubs, but the city's history also incorporates rockabilly, rock and roll and soul. Seen as the gateway to the Delta region, Beale Street attracted blues musicians in the 1950s from all over the Southern states. There were regular performances from Bobby "Blue" Bland, Sleepy John Estes and Muddy Waters, plus, of course, B.B. King, after whom a two-mile stretch of Third Street is named, and whose Blues Club dominates the top end of Beale Street.

As well as blues, Memphis specialised in the

rockabilly style of artists like Elvis Presley, Carl Perkins, Roy Orbison and Johnny Cash. All of them recorded prolifically with Sam Phillips at his Sun Records studio, which can also be toured at 706, Union Avenue. With Elvis Presley and Cash, rural music became sharpened by the grittier, more urban environment of Memphis. In the end, Presley became more of a mainstream rock and roll or pop artist, while Cash was seen as a pioneer of Country music. Presley, although living most of his adult life in Memphis, was originally from northern Mississippi. Cash was originally from Arkansas.

The first thing that happened as we hit the world famous blues thoroughfare, which featured a motorcycle gathering on that particular evening, was that my eye was attracted to a shop called A. Schwab. This was irresistible, because it reminded me of my dearest ever friend, Albrecht Schwab, whom I met in Germany in 1969. We stayed close for many years, but Albrecht died of lung cancer in 2010. It kind of felt like a homage to Albrecht, as we trawled the shelves of the ancient shop, which has remained virtually unchanged since it first opened in 1876. It is actually the only original business remaining on Beale Street. It specializes in historic bits and pieces, ranging from regional arts and crafts, to "magic potions", to Memphis brands such as Sun Studio, Hi Records and Stax. Albrecht would have loved it.

In contrast to Nashville's Broadway, we found that every bar on Beale Street into which we put our heads contained a smoking-hot and pretty authentic-sounding local blues band, although most of them, of course, were playing mainly standards and covers for the tourist audiences. Still, it felt like we had done the Memphis experience and enjoyed all of it.

STAX OF CASH

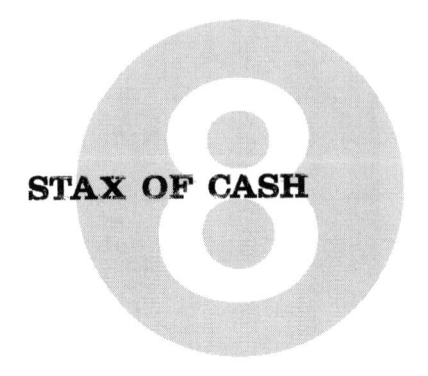

When it comes to shopping. I'm a bit of a cliché male. It may be apparent already that this whole trip was one enormous piece of self-indulgence for me. Birgit probably couldn't have cared less about the majority of music-based activities we had been pursuing, but because she is such a kind person, she was happy to go along with my whims. To even things out a little, the following day in Memphis was designated as a shopping day. Personally, I would be quite happy never to enter a shop again as long as I live, but the plan today was to search for lovely clothes for granddaughter Ella, and as far as Ella is concerned, there are no sacrifices that I will not make. You may have noticed that this had developed into something of a leit-motif of the trip.

Birgit had made some enquiries and been told the name and address of a "designer outlet" specialising in children's garments, so off we set to find it. It didn't seem a particularly challenging task on the face of it, but it turned out to be less easy than anticipated, largely, once again, as a result of the failings of our Tom Tom. When our little friend confidently announced that we had reached our destination, we found ourselves at a desolate crossroads which featured, on its four corners, a pizza takeaway, a hairdresser, a gas station and a hardware store. Of designer kiddies' items there was no sign. Yes, it was that old Crossroads thing again. Nobody we asked had even heard of the place we were looking for, so we did a bit of googling, which told us that we were exactly where we were meant to be.

Clearly, the shop didn't exist, so we set off to look for an alternative we had identified. This experience was even less productive, as it took us four times up and down a busy highway for several miles but once again produced no results. Finally accepting that our mission was doomed to failure, we eventually spotted a branch of Macy's. This department store was one of those strange places containing a series of mini-shops featuring famous brand names, and we proceeded to spend nearly two hours as the sole customers in the basement children's department. And you know what? I loved every minute of it, and we emerged clutching bundles of sweet little dresses and dungarees. The shop assistant was startled to have any customers at all and nearly fainted when she heard our accents and realized we were exotic creatures from another land.

Right, that was that out of the way, now it was time to return to pandering to Oliver's musical desires. There was one more studio that had to be toured, and that was Stax. Epitomised by Otis Redding, the Stax Sound is unique and instantly recognisable, but I knew little about the history of the label. Housed in a reconstructed version of the original studio, the museum vividly tells a classic music "rags to riches to rags" story.

A company called Satellite Records was founded in October 1957 by Jim Stewart, a banker who was also a Country fiddle player. He took as his model Sam Phillips, who had made a fortune in the same city from producing Elvis Presley. Despite having neither expertise nor experience, Stewart cast himself as a record producer and came up with a Country track called "Blue Roses". Needing to upgrade his equipment, Stewart persuaded his bank clerk sister Estelle Axton to invest in the company, which she duly did by mortgaging her house.

Stax Records was born in 1960, when Estelle remortgaged once more, so that the studio could upgrade to bigger and better premises. To this end, they bought an old cinema, the Capitol, on McLemore Avenue in Memphis. This was when they decided to amalgamate the first two letters of their names (Stewart and Axton) to make the title Stax.

Doing all the work themselves, the pair converted the huge room with partitions. As it had been a cinema, the floor was slanted, but they retained this feature, unique to any recording studio, and it helped create the signature Stax sound by deadening any echos. To make sure there was still a regular inflow of cash, the Satellite record store was incorporated into the old cinema foyer. Thus the building became a place for all the local musicians, including guitarist Steve Cropper, to hang out, socialise and create music. The new studio's first single was called "Cause I Love You", by Rufus and Carla Thomas. It had local success and attracted the attention of Jerry Wexler of Atlantic Records, which soon afterwards became the distributor for all Stax product.

Many songs were recorded at Stax, using the house band of Booker T. Jones, Steve Cropper, Al Jackson, and Donald "Duck" Dunn (who replaced Lewie Steinberg in 1964). The instrumental "Green Onions" was developed on a whim, when they were needing a B-Side for their proposed single "Behave Yourself", which was actually only created when the band was bored while waiting for a singer called Billy Lee Riley to arrive for a session. The next morning, Steve Cropper took a tape of the Hammond instrumental into a local radio station, which played it five times in a row, starting an immediate buzz, which ended in "Green Onions" becoming a hit that is still regularly played to this day. Oddly, though, despite being popular in dance clubs, it didn't become a chart hit in Europe until 1979, when it was featured on the soundtrack of the film "Quadrophenia".

The story of how Otis Redding joined Stax is extraordinary. A band called Johnny Jenkins and the Pinetoppers were in the studio, recording an instrumental to cash in on the success of "Green Onions". Redding was their chauffeur, and when the recording didn't work out well, he was allowed to do some vocals. No one at the time knew that Redding would become Stax's greatest asset.

In the early 1960s, the Stax studio went through a particularly fruitful period, with records by the Mar-Keys, Booker T and The MGs, William Bell, Rufus Thomas, Carla Thomas and Otis Redding. The label also released songs by Sam and Dave, who were licensed to Stax by Atlantic Records. But things were changing and racial tension was beginning to brew in Memphis and elsewhere. Stax was different, a fully-integrated multicultural collective concentrating on making music regardless of race or colour.

As Stewart became more skilled as an engineer and producer, Axton continued to manage the store and, as hit followed hit, Stewart was finally able to quit his day job at the bank. The new promotions manager, Al Bell, then set up a game-changing tour of Europe for a package starring Otis Redding, Eddie Floyd, Carla Thomas, the MGs and the Mar-Keys. Most of them had previously never even stepped outside Memphis. Stax records had become very popular in Europe, and European audiences were as enthused by Stax as American teenagers had been when the British Invasion first came to America. In Europe, race was a less important issue. The music was seen as authentic and the musicians as stars.

Just as had happened before with the blues, Stax's success in Europe raised its profile in the the U.S., and in a pivotal move, Otis Redding was booked to perform at the Monterey Pop Festival in 1967. The hippie audience, primarily there to see white psychedelic acts, were knocked out by the soulful energy of Redding and the Mar-Keys. Jimi Hendrix was another black artist who achieved his major breakthrough at Monterey.

Stax seemed to be going through a golden period, but then tragedy struck. Otis Redding recorded "Dock of the Bay", probably his best-known song, in November 1967 and straight afterwards took off with his band in a private plane to perform a show in Madison, Wisconsin. Shortly before it was due to land in Madison, the plane developed battery problems and plunged into an ice-cold lake, killing Redding and four members of the Mar-Keys, as well as an assistant and the pilot. In April 1968, Martin Luther King was assassinated at the Lorraine Motel. This was particularly painful for Stax, because the Lorraine had been a regular meeting place for its artists and employees, both black and white. The rioting in the streets following King's murder thankfully left the Stax building unscathed, but the atmosphere had been changed forever.

Atlantic Records (Stax's distributor) was sold to Warner Brothers in 1967. Jim Stewart made several attempts to negotiate a new distribution deal, but nothing worked out with either company. Stax asked Warner for their master tapes back but Warner refused to return them.

Al Bell was made vice president of Stax after Estelle Axton retired in 1969. It was clear that Stax, having lost its back catalogue, needed a new start. During that year, the label entered into a busy period of creating new recordings in an attempt to establish a new catalogue. The period was aptly named the Soul Explosion, producing twenty-seven albums and thirty singles over just eight months.

Isaac Hayes, who had been a songwriter for Stax for many years, was given the artistic freedom to create an album in any form he wanted, which led to the release of "Hot Buttered Soul", an album that was on the face of it uncommercial, as each track was at least five minutes long. Nonetheless, it was an immediate success, selling over three million copies in 1969.

Hayes was Stax's big new star, enabling the label and studio to expand, even recording at places other than McLemore Avenue, but inevitably the "family" atmosphere changed for the worse as things became more corporate and businesslike and Stax became less of a co-operative run by creative artists. Black music was suddenly thriving, along with the Black Pride movement. Bell was determined to expand nationwide and to that end, sent a massive package of Stax artists including the Staple Singers, Rufus Thomas, the Bar-Kays and, of course, Isaac Hayes, to play a festival in Los Angeles in August 1972. A documentary and live recording of the concert was released and soon sold 500,000 copies, giving Stax the wider attention it had sought.

More clouds were on the horizon, though. Stax's security man was caught at Memphis Airport with 130,000 dollars in cash in his bag. This incident, of course, drew the attention of the tax authorities, who began to investigate the company. Stax had had a distribution arrangement with CBS, but it fell through in 1972, meaning that, although the label's songs were in demand, they were unable to get them to the customers. As a result of this, Stax found itself deep in debt.

As if things couldn't get worse, conspiracy theorists then had a field day with the murder of the MGs' drummer Al Jackson on October 1, 1975. He was found at his home, having been shot in the back five times, with his wife tied up and screaming in the road outside. No perpetrator has ever been arrested for the murder, but there are several intriguing complicating factors. First, Jackson's wife Barbara had herself shot her husband in the chest earlier in the year after a vicious argument, but she was acquitted on the grounds of extreme provocation - Jackson had earlier threatened her and fired his pistol into the floor. And secondly, rumours abound that the murder could have had something to do with the litigation and the chaos surrounding the imminent demise of Stax. As the case has never been solved, all of these factors remain mysteries.

On December 19, 1975, everyone in the Stax building was ordered to leave immediately, as federal marshals invaded the studio. The old cinema and its contents were impounded and Stax was forced into involuntary bankruptcy. Various creditors had sued the company for money it didn't have. Al Bell was forced from the building at gunpoint and the bank took everything in it, including all the master tapes. Stax, the centre of the community that had provided work for so many local people, was no more, and Bell was convinced that it was because the white power structure in Memphis resented a predominantly black business being so successful.

The studio remained empty and abandoned until 1981, when it was sold to the Church of God in Christ for a mere ten dollars. Nothing came of their plans and the building, having fallen into total disrepair, was eventually demolished in 1989, with a historical marker being the only sign that it had ever existed. At around the same time, the surrounding area was experiencing serious deprivation and the strong community feel had all but disappeared. But there was a reluctance to see the legacy die altogether, and a community group, some philanthropic financiers and people who had been connected to Stax found a way to help regenerate the area. The Soulsville Foundation was set up in order to provide mentoring and music-related education for local youngsters, at the same time creating a museum telling the story of Stax. This is what can be visited today.

The studio tour was a more formal and less emotional experience than visiting Muscle Shoals, because it's much more of a hands-off type museum which you move through at some speed. Also, it isn't the original studio in any real sense, as it has been reconstructed. Still, it was highly educational and revelatory to find out just how many brilliant records had been made there. In the main studio itself, the Hammond organ, the amps and the drums are encased in plexiglass and you aren't allowed to touch them. Following us around was a group of middle-aged gentleman, one of whom kept referring to his mates "Duck" and "Steve" (one can only assume Dunn and Cropper) as if he was one of their best friends:

"Yeah, well, of course, when I was recording here with Duck, blah blah …"

I didn't pluck up courage to interrupt the conversation and enquire who he was, but I wish I had. The tour ended with a few minutes spent ogling Isaac Hayes' gold Cadillac, pretty much the ultimate in Rock Star accoutrements. Afterwards, we wondered round the area and it seemed perfectly pleasant, but later I spoke to someone who knows Memphis very well and who assured me that it was still a very dangerous neighbourhood. It didn't feel that way.

Back at the Mansion, we asked our hosts if they could recommend a Mexican restaurant. Indeed they could but, guess what, it couldn't be reached on foot. We Ubered our way there and were rewarded by gigantic tumblers of frozen Margarita to accompany the requisite shrimp enchiladas. Thus it was with a light heart and a spinning head that I pressed the Uber button on my phone, only to discover that it didn't work. Extraordinarily, the restaurant had no Wi-Fi. A kind waitress offered to call a car for us, but couldn't get her phone to work either. In the end, she called her boyfriend, who was at home. He, in turn, ordered the car to come and pick us up and we paid the waitress the money so she could pass it on to her boyfriend. It did all work in the end, but it was a tense half an hour or so.

Our target the following morning was a place that I had been recommended by a friend before setting off. It was Johnny Cash's childhood home, situated north of Memphis, over the border in Arkansas. This turned out to be another day of adventure and excitement. We were, according to the Sat Nav, about ten miles away from the Dyess Colony where Johnny grew up, when we were suddenly instructed to leave the highway and take a road which was so insignificant that it hardly seemed to qualify as a road at all. Great clouds of dust blew up into the air from our tyres as we began to bump along a rough track that stretched endlessly across the completely flat, featureless landscape. "This can't be right," we agreed, but the little machine on the dashboard seemed determined to contradict us.

Very occasionally, we would pass a scruffy homestead, out of which slavering dogs would rush, rearing up against the car and barking wildly at us. Threatening-looking farmers, no doubt toting firearms, I assumed, would stare at us in an unfriendly manner.

"Okay, so this is what's going to happen," I thought. "The tyres are going to be punctured by sharp thorns and we are going to be killed either by being shot by the landowners, or by being bitten by venomous snakes. Either way, we'll die."

Of any other form of civilisation there was no sign, so all we could do was trustfully continue to follow the instructions. Occasionally, we would reach a deserted crossroads, where the brown track would split in a barely discernible way. One thing that was quite clear was that no way were we being led to anything that could possibly be a tourist attraction. Hearts in mouths, we agreed that we had finally ridden our luck too far and were about to be punished. Eventually, however, we spotted a cluster of small houses in the distance and entered something that seemed straight out of that wonderful film The Last Picture Show. Indeed, the centre of this little settlement was actually something that seemed like a little theatre. This turned out to be the visitor centre for the Dyess Colony.

This extraordinary community was established in 1934 as a part of an agricultural resettlement programme initiated by President Franklin Roosevelt's administration. It's named after its first administrator, William Dyess. He'd originally moved to Arkansas to work for a company doing work on the levees. His plan, conceived in 1930, was for a colony of small subsistence farms. The purpose was to tame the vast expanses of wild swamplands and to make then not only habitable for humans, but also usable as farmland. The colony was laid out with a small town in the centre and family-run farmsteads stretching out into the surroundings. The first thirteen families arrived in October 1934, but sadly Mr Dyess never go to see the fruits of his project, because he died in a plane crash in 1936.

The Dyess Colony was a unique and highly innovative social experiment, giving almost five hundred deprived farmers the opportunity for a new start in life. Johnny's parents, Ray and Carrie Cash, were among the families who travelled from all over Arkansas to be part of the Dyess Colony. The Cashes moved to Dyess in March 1935 with their five children, including the three-year old JR, as Johnny had actually been named. With no money needing to be deposited, the family received twenty acres of fertile land and a five-room house in which to live. The only problem was that it was their job to tame the land and make it cultivatable, a huge physical challenge requiring much hardship and dedication.

Two more Cash children were born in Dyess. The Cash home is now one of the few houses remaining in the former colony. Johnny lived in Dyess until he graduated from high school in 1950. His music, including songs such as "Pickin' Time" and "Five Feet High and Rising" was greatly influenced by his hard upbringing and environment. The latter song was inspired by the floods that engulfed the home at least twice.

Charming local residents, who were volunteer guides at the visitor centre, welcomed us as we arrived and smiled ruefully at our tale of how we managed to find them.

"We keep telling the Google Maps people that the roads they send people down don't actually exist as roads, but they haven't done anything about it. Last month an entire coach load of Irish tourists tried to come that way after a heavy rainstorm. The coach got bogged down up to its wheel arches and they all had to be rescued and taken to a hotel. You were lucky."

A tiny minibus driven by a very chatty guide from the Arkansas State University took us the two miles or so to cabin number 266, which was where Johnny had grown up with his family. Once again, I found myself overwhelmed with emotion as Birgit and I were allowed to sit together on the little swing chair on the patio, where Johnny himself would have sat as a child. Similarly to the Elvis birthplace, the house has been restored but not tampered with, so that you can walk through it and experience it precisely as young JR Cash would have. It was very moving to reflect how here, once again, a global superstar had emerged from the humblest possible origins. Nowadays the project is still supported by the Cash family, and Roseanne Cash recorded a video for her song "The Road Home" there. Each year, a fundraising Johnny Cash Heritage Festival is held adjacent to the home. In 2019, it featured Roseanne, together with Marty Stuart, among others.

Also in the minibus was a young Welsh lady and her boyfriend, who were being giving VIP treatment by the Arkansas Tourist Board. Feeling mildly jealous, I inquired as to what her rôle was. "I'm a travel writer," she explained. "I'm planning to write a piece about visiting Arkansas." In order to do this, it emerged that she and her boyfriend were being driven around the state for a week by a guide and put up in smart hotels. I persuaded her to give me her business card and, on returning home, looked her up. It turned out that she runs a pretty bog-standard travel blog, such as you or I or anybody else could set up in five minutes, and which is unlikely to be read by more than a few people. Basically, she had pulled off a very impressive scam and gained herself a free holiday. Nice work if you can get it.

Back in the centre of Dyess, still paranoid about preserving the integrity of the hire car, I had an enjoyable, if slightly messy, half hour making use of the self-service car wash facility, which is actually a museum piece but still in working order and cost only one dollar. In the town hall next to the theatre we found a highly informative museum explaining the history of the colony and its people. Here you can hear Johnny Cash's music as it is placed in context. It's a super cool place indeed.

PARSONS NOSE

It was time to move on, because the road trip was gradually nearing its end. I was determined to visit Loretta Lynn's Ranch because it lay more or less en route from Dyess to Nashville, from where we were due to fly home. In preparing the trip, I had decided to go for one final nice hotel so that the journey would end in a happy memory. Studying the map revealed the name of a small town positioned in a convenient place. The town was called Parsons and the hotel that I identified was called The Parsons Inn. In my deluded state, this conjured up ideas of an idyllic English village such as you might find in Midsomer Murders, with a thatched village inn and a country parson in a dog collar pedalling down the road on his bicycle.

The Parsons Inn didn't have many reviews on Trip Advisor, but those that there were, were uniformly positive and the overall rating was four stars. The general consensus was that it was a pleasant environment to spend a night in a nice small town, so I booked it online. It was a long drive and it seemed to take forever to get there. We stopped for lunch in a godforsaken truckstop, where we indulged in one of the least gourmet meals you could ever imagine, courtesy of a dingy Subway franchise. If you aren't familiar with the culture of Subway, the array of soggy breads and reconstituted fillings is so baffling that we almost gave up, and hugely annoyed all the people behind us in the queue as we made our deliberations. As for our naive attempts to order a cup of tea to go with the "sub", they were clearly doomed to failure from the start.

Eventually we reached Parsons City Limits and then, shortly afterwards, we reached the City Limits again on the way out. There had been no sign of our hotel, so we turned around and drove back into the centre of Parsons.

Still seeing no indication of any hotels, we decided to pull into a gas station and ask where it was. There I found two middle-aged ladies behind the counter.

"Good afternoon," I said. "I wonder if you could tell me where the Parsons Inn is?"

"The Parsons Inn?"

"That's right, we think it must be here somewhere."

The two ladies looked at each other knowingly.

"Sure it's here somewhere, but you won't be staying there," said one of them to me.

"Yes, we will. I've already booked and we just need to know where it is, please."

"You won't be staying there," she repeated, while her colleague nodded in agreement.

"I'm sorry, I don't understand what you mean."

"When you get there, you will understand, believe me."

"Why, is there a problem with it?"

The two ladies again turned to each other and then back to me.

"Drugs," they said in unison and then, after a short pause, "drugs and guns."

This was indeed worrying, but I wasn't going to take their word for it. To be frank, I had been rather proud of finding this place and I certainly wasn't going to change my mind without good cause.

"Well, thank you, but I would like to check it out, so could you tell me where it is?"

"Sure, it's just next door, but you won't be staying there."

Immediately next to the gas station was a car breaker's yard and a small potholed alley next to it led to the Parsons Inn. The immediate thought on seeing it was, "Oh God, Bates Motel". Round a scruffy yard were a series of dilapidated white-coloured bungalows with various dodgy looking people hanging around. I identified the office and proceeded to check in with a pleasant gentleman behind the desk. Several of the reviews had referred to a nice family taking on the inn and turning it round. He was reasonably welcoming but something in his manner told me that English tourists probably weren't their normal day-to-day clientèle.

It is now time to admit that I didn't tell Birgit about what the lady in the garage had said. I can be relatively stubborn when I've made a decision or a choice and (surely the only thing I can possibly have in common with Theresa May), I tend to stick to decisions unless they are blatantly stupid or absolutely unavoidable. As it stood, it seemed to me that a bed was a bed. It was reasonably cheap and we were only going to be there for one night, so what the heck?

The look on Birgit's face as we inspected our accommodation was quite a picture. We opened the rickety door to be assailed by a deeply pungent smell. It was clear that this was a smoking room, despite the fact that we had booked a non-smoking one. Well, to be fair, there was a large sign saying No Smoking, but a large sign doesn't actually guarantee that the people before you haven't just ignored it and continued to puff away. The plastic bath was scarred with brown burn marks from where people had obviously been lying in the bath and leaving their lit cigarettes on the edge of it. Clearly we wouldn't be able to stay here, but for some reason, neither of us had the courage to take that decision. We sat down on the two queen-size beds and pronounced them reasonably comfortable. Birgit's inspection of the towels and sheets found them to be clean, so a brief conversation led us to the conclusion that we might as well just put up with it and move on in the morning. Yes, it was disappointing that we wouldn't have a cosy last night, but maybe the airport hotel the next day would turn out to be okay.

The next question was where to eat. Again, we both had a romantic notion that there might be a lovely restaurant where we could bring our trip to a pleasant conclusion. I returned to the office and asked the owner for a recommendation. He revealed that, a short drive up the road, there was a baked potato shop. It wasn't quite what we had had in mind but we concluded that a baked potato would be likely to be a lot healthier than most things we had eaten in the last few days. We arrived once again at the Parsons crossroads (yes, crossroads are definitely a recurring theme) turned right and parked up in front of Prater's Taters, where the teenager mopping the floor gave us a withering glance and announced that they were closed. This was 8 p.m. It was becoming clear that Parsons wasn't just a one-horse town, it was a no-horse town. There didn't even seem to be anywhere to get a beer.

"Can you recommend anywhere else?"

"Well, there's the Dairy King ice cream parlour."

This wasn't what we had had in mind either, but as it seemed to be the only option, we drove back to the centre and parked up outside what appeared to be the social centre of Parsons. We were the only vehicle that wasn't a huge pickup truck. It seemed that Friday nights were the time for the locals to congregate and sit in the back of their pickups scoffing ice cream sundaes. It turned out they did burgers as well, so our romantic gourmet meal consisted of sitting in the car, dripping burger grease all over our clothes and spooning synthetic ice cream into our mouths.

As Parsons seemed to offer no other possibilities of entertainment, we decided to opt for an early night, but as we walked across the yard, I was becoming more and more apprehensive. There were strange characters loitering about and it was clear that we were potential sitting ducks. I know I probably shouldn't have allowed preconceptions to take over but those two words Drugs and Guns that the ladies at the petrol station had uttered had spooked me more than I realised. I was trying to find a way to get round to suggesting to Birgit that we should leave. In my mind, two innocent-looking European tourists lugging huge wheelie suitcases into a room with no security would potentially be a tempting target for anybody wanting to rob them. Most American hotels have doors with several substantial locks, but this door was a flimsy wooden affair with a simple and very loose Yale lock. One quick kick would have it down in seconds. But by the time these thoughts were crystalising in my mind, I had already undressed and got into bed.

Then Birgit gave me all the excuse I needed. I was just switching on my Kindle when I heard a scream:

"Oh my God, it's a cockroach!" she yelled.

True enough, a large black beetle-like creature was crawling its way across the floor and up the leg of Birgit's bed.

"That's it, we're going," I cried, secretly pleased that I now had more obvious grounds then cowardice for the decision. Something else had struck me too. That horrible stench hadn't just been of tobacco remnants but had more of a chemical element to it. Of course, the room must have been recently fumigated, and the smell must have been the chemicals used.

I threw on my clothes, because it was already half past nine, and if we were going to find somewhere else to stay, we needed to get a move on, or else risk sleeping in the car. Feeling slightly guilty, I returned to the office and broke the news to the owner. He actually didn't seem too surprised, just rather disappointed. He half-heartedly tried to convince me that the creature had been harmless.

"Here in Tennessee we have a lot of beetles, you know. I'm sure it's not a cockroach."

"I understand," I replied, "but I'm afraid I'm not enough of an entomologist to be able to distinguish between different types of bug, and ..." (sneakily trying to shift the blame) "... my wife isn't willing to stay here."

It seemed extra-inappropriate to ask him to recommend another hotel, so we returned once more to the gas station where, not unnaturally, the two ladies were convulsed with hysterical laughter.

"We told you you wouldn't be staying!"

"You did, but I didn't believe you. Now we need your help. Are there any other hotels nearby?"

"Only one, it's three miles up the road."

Predictably, on a day like this when you're on a roll of things going wrong, that damn cursed crossroads let us down again, and we drove for miles and miles in the wrong direction, before admitting to ourselves that we'd clearly taken the wrong road, and returning, yet again, to the centre of Parsons. True enough, three miles along the correct road, we found what seemed to be a reasonable motel, but it was suspiciously dark. Looking through the locked lobby door, I could see an old lady asleep in a rocking chair. Yes, memories of a particular Hitchcock movie once again seemed to be particularly apt. I tapped hesitantly on the window and her eyes opened. She unlocked the door, beckoned me in in a friendly way and asked to see my reservation.

"Oh, we haven't reserved. We were hoping that you might have a room free."

"You ain't reserved? I thought you must be the last two guests I was waiting up for. I'm sorry, but we're fully booked."

This was astonishing. It was hard to fathom what attractions Parsons might have that would have caused such popularity.

"Really?"

"Yes, this is our busiest weekend of the year, what with the Gun Convention and the World War Two Re-enactment Society Conference."

I was temporarily lost for words but did manage to gasp out a plea for any other hotels in the area.

"No, sir, this is the only hotel for miles. You'll have to drive to the Interstate, where you may find a hotel with rooms to spare."

"Where is the Interstate?"

"Carry on along this road for thirty miles and you'll get there soon enough."

The lady then kindly phoned someone she knew in the Days Inn on the Interstate and established that they had rooms to spare, but the nail-biting wasn't quite over yet, because they weren't able to guarantee that they wouldn't have all been taken by the time we got there. It was a nervous and rather frightening drive along a long, dark road, only punctuated by the occasional headlights of huge trucks thundering past us in the opposite direction.

All was well. Yet another charming Indian family was running the Days Inn and we managed to grab the last room. Inserting the earplugs to keep out the traffic noise, we were finally able to relax.

In the morning, I was badly in need of a bath, but a bath in an American hotel is never straightforward. More often than not there's no plug, and this was indeed the case at the Days Inn. Luckily, I was experienced in these matters and able to stick my heel in the plughole while the bath filled up. That is something that only works if there is an efficient mixer tap attached to the bath, because you have to be actually in it as it fills up, rather than doing the traditional sticking of the toe into the water to check its temperature. You could receive a scalded bottom if you didn't pay attention.

The reason for so many hotel bathrooms not having bath plugs is that most people prefer to take showers. I am familiar with the arguments for and against baths and showers, as I have had such discussions many times with my German friends. In their opinion, baths are wasteful because they use more water than showers. It is also argued that all you do is redistribute the dirt and sweat from one part of your body to the rest of it, because it disappears into the water and then clings back onto your skin. I fear this is probably true.

My counter-argument is that showering is also wasteful, because most of the water passes straight past you and out through the bottom of the shower. It's also very difficult to avoid getting your hair wet if you don't want it to be wet. Above all, if you are unfamiliar with the shower, it is well-nigh impossible to avoid being either given first degree burns or frozen half to death because, particularly in hotels, the mechanism for setting the shower water at a tolerable temperature is almost impossible to understand. There are never any signs to tell you which taps are hot and which are cold, or whether the temperature increases or decreases by turning them to the left or the right. The trendier and more modern the design of the mechanism is, the more likely it is to cause confusion. Sometimes the levers even pull towards you or push away from you. The only way you can experiment and find out how they work is to strip off and go underneath them, risking discomfort and even injury. When faced with situations where a shower is unavoidable, I tend to find myself standing outside it, reaching into the cubicle and drenching my sleeves in the process of finding out how to operate the infernal machine. That's why I still prefer a bath, even if I have to stick my heel in the plughole, causing a round red and white blob on the bottom of my foot.

END OF THE ROAD

The road to Nashville the next morning took us directly past the entrance to Loretta Lynn's Ranch at Hurricane Mills. I had been hesitant about visiting this place, because I'm not that bothered about Country music and it could have been tacky in the extreme, but something about the mere word "ranch" was enough to sway the decision. Brought up on the Lone Ranger, Champion The Wonder Horse and Roy Rogers, I've always had an affectionate and sentimental attachment to the cowboy genre, and the ranch duly lived up to the highest expectations.

Loretta Lynn (born Loretta Webb in 1932, in Butcher

Hollow, Kentucky) is probably best known as the subject of "The Coal Miner's Daughter", the 1980 Michael Apted-produced film of her life, starring Tommy Lee Jones and Sissy Spacek. Spacek won an Oscar for her portrayal of Lynn, and the film even featured a cameo from Levon Helm of The Band. It's a classic tale of huge success attained from humble beginnings with a lot of trouble along the way - an "American Dream" in fact.

Lynn grew up in a small wooden hut in a poor Appalachian coal-mining town. Two of the eight children in the family went on to forge professional careers as singers, having been brought up singing in church. Loretta's sister is Crystal Gayle. When Loretta married Oliver Lynn in 1948, it was rumoured by some that she was only thirteen, but in fact she was just under sixteen. Nevertheless, she still managed to give birth to four children before she was twenty. "Mooney", as Oliver was known, bought Loretta her first guitar and music was a constant in her life, but it wasn't until 1960 that she released her first single, "I'm a Honky Tonk Girl," which became a hit, as a result of Mooney and Loretta travelling round the country promoting it to radio stations.

The couple moved to Nashville and Loretta began performing at the Grand Ole Opry, leading in turn to being signed by Decca and achieving a run of Country Chart hits, including "Blue Kentucky Girl" and "Wine, Women and Song". She became good friends with Patsy Cline, who helped her out with the business side of the industry, but the relationship was cut short by Cline's death in a plane crash in 1963.

Finding time to give birth to more children, in the shape of twin daughters in 1964, she started writing her own material as well as covering the songs of others. Her themes tended to tackle the problems of women and mothers in a humorous way, but she also wrote an anti-Vietnam War song called "Dear Uncle Sam". The song "Coal Miner's Daughter", on which the film was based, was a Number 1 hit in 1970. During the 1970s, she teamed up for a succession of hits with her friend Conway Twitty. There is a section of the Loretta Lynn Museum devoted to this productive relationship.

Loretta continued to have mainstream chart hits, some of which, such as "Rated X" and "Out of My Head and Back in My Bed" (both of them Number 1 hits), were considered rather risqué. Her first autobiography caused controversy by revealing her difficult and violent relationship with her husband. It was characterised by cruelty and brutality, aided by Mooney's alcoholism.

The couple faced more sadness when their son Jack drowned while trying to wade across a river on his horse. Lynn herself was a true Country superstar, talked about in the same breath as Tammy Wynette and Dolly Parton, with both of whom she worked, but Mooney was becoming frail and afflicted with both diabetes and a heart condition, so Loretta stepped back to care for him. She was inducted into the Country Music Hall of Fame in 1988, but Mooney died in 1996. Their marriage had lasted nearly fifty years.

After a few low-key years, Loretta, by now aged 73, struck up an unexpected musical relationship with Jack White of the White Stripes. She even performed live with them, and White ended up producing her album, Van Lear Rose, which turned out to be a smash hit, winning them two Grammys. White famously described Loretta as "the greatest female singer-songwriter of the last century."

In 2010, she received a Grammy Lifetime Achievement Award and later, Barack Obama bestowed on her the Presidential Medal of Freedom, but around the same time, her eldest daughter, Betty Sue, died, aged 64. Not even this prevented the octogenarian Lynn from continuing to write and record, and in 2016 she was back at the top of the Country charts with her album "Full Circle".

On May 4, 2017, by now aged 84, she suffered a stroke at home on her ranch and was taken to a Nashville hospital. In addition to this, she fractured her hip, allegedly by tripping over her dog. But we had chosen a particularly serendipitous time to visit the ranch because, amazingly, Loretta had just released a new album that very week. Indeed, it had been launched in Ernest Tubb's record store in Nashville while we were there. To come up with a new album (her forty-first) at the age of 86, produced by John Carter Cash, was a pretty impressive achievement. Not that I would have bought it, of course, but we did spend several hours admiring her stage costumes and roomfuls of memorabilia. Loretta is clearly a devoted hoarder of every possible knick-knack. A video screen showed extracts from "The Coal Miner's Daughter" and some of her duets with Conway Twitty.

Afterwards, we attempted to find a trail to walk, but it only lasted a few hundred metres. Walking is probably anathema to most of the museum visitors, but a large part of the ranch is dedicated to what they call a RV Park, where people pitch up in their gigantic mobile homes, many of them the size of an actual house. The rest of the ranch is just as you would imagine, gentle hills and forests with wooden buildings (selling souvenirs, naturally) and golden palaminos trotting across the fields. All in all, visiting the ranch was a total pleasure and once again, we learnt a huge amount about the local culture in the space of a few hours.

It was time to think about heading back to the airport to drop off the car, but the route to the airport took us around the periphery of Nashville. Most American cities have extensive highways circling round them and I have to confess I find them particularly terrifying. This is because, more often than not, they have five or even six lanes on each side and drivers switch from one to the other at great speed, with little in the way of indication. Thus it was that, for the fifty minutes or so it took us to get to the airport, I had to keep my eyes firmly closed.

There is something about American lorries that is particularly intimidating. Their size is absolutely vast and they tend to have wobbly trailers attached to the back and enormous periscope-shaped exhaust pipes protruding from the top. The drivers can be particularly frightening-looking. So huge are the trucks that their drivers are completely dwarfed in their cabs and it's hard to see how they can possibly be in full control, especially as they are normally smoking and leaning casualty against the window.

People have often asked me where my motorway phobia originated and, although I can't specifically pin it down, there are two incidents which, I think, contributed to it. The first one occurred when I was in my late teens and hitch-hiking through a town called Stratton St Margaret, near Swindon. As the traffic slowed and it was clear that there had recently been a crash on the road, the driver called out to me, "Don't look!"

"Don't look at what?" I asked, as I of course looked.

A tiny sports car, probably an MG or something like that, had crashed head-on into a large lorry and had virtually disappeared underneath it. All that could be seen was the extreme rear of the car and the exhaust pipe. One can only assume that the driver had been decapitated at the very least. It was too late for me not to look and the memory has stayed with me ever since.

Even more pertinent to attempting to negotiate the highways of Tennessee, even as a passenger, was a film I saw in 1972. Called "Duel", this was one of the earliest movies directed by Steven Spielberg, and the sole storyline consists of a couple in a car being stalked, followed and generally harassed across a desert by a gigantic American truck with no discernible driver. It has to be said that it is indeed a fantastic film that I actually watched twice, because the plot is so mysterious that it's not entirely clear, on first viewing, what is happening. Well, actually, on second viewing it's even less clear. But I'm pretty sure that the truck in "Duel" bears considerable responsibility for my phobia.

Before we made it to the airport, we had to confront another matter that had been causing a certain amount of anxiety. We had agreed to return the car full of petrol - er - "gas", so it was necessary to identify a gas station as close as possible to the airport. The problem was that it was not permitted simply to insert the nozzle, squirt until the tank was full and then pay for what we had put in. For some reason, it was necessary to press a button in advance saying how much was required. Of course, we didn't know how much we required, so had to fill up in three separate ten-dollar increments, something that caused considerable amusement and also some impatience among the other drivers queuing to use the pumps.

Thankfully, when we handed the car back, the lady with the Ed Sheeran fixation was absent, and, as promised, the guy collecting it from us showed absolutely no interest in whether we had added any bumps and scrapes to it. Calling an Uber to take us to the hotel caused the usual grief, because I had to log on to the airport Wi-Fi and then hotfoot it across to the pickup point, where there was no Wi-Fi available. Somehow, we managed to find each other and were taken to something called an Extended Stay, which seemed, on the booking website, to be a souped-up hotel. We hoped it might be near a nice restaurant for a final blow-out, prior to the flight early the next morning.

As we neared the hotel, we soon knew that we were doomed. It was a typical American suburb with absolutely no facilities for pedestrians, so getting to a restaurant wasn't going to be feasible. We also briefly thought about cooking for ourselves, as Extended Stay rooms contain a small kitchenette, but we discovered later that this was an incredibly complicated procedure, involving hiring pots and pans from the establishment.

That we were not going to have any kind of relationship with the hotel staff soon became clear. As we negotiated the door (one of those irritating ones which only open outwards and therefore make it nearly impossible to get through with a suitcase), we saw in front of us a long flight of stairs leading up to the rooms. In an attempt to check in, we had a few questions to ask and the response was quite astonishing. With an almost insolent use of the word "Sir", this was the response we got to our various questions:

"Good afternoon. Is there anywhere nearby we can

go out to eat?"

"No, Sir."

"Is there maybe a shop nearby where we could buy some food to cook ourselves?"

"No, Sir."

"Is there an elevator so we can avoid those stairs?"

"No, Sir."

"Is there anyone who could help us lug our heavy suitcases up that flight of stairs?"

"No, Sir."

"Could we have some milk to make tea with?"

"No, Sir."

"Will there be a hot breakfast?"

"No, Sir."

"Will there be anything more than these muffins for breakfast?"

"No, Sir."

"Would it be possible for you to order us a taxi?"

"No, Sir."

No further engagement was offered, so we dragged our bags up to the room and accepted that the evening would be spent desperately searching for something to watch on television and eating the few remaining granola bars and brown bananas that we had stolen from previous hotels.

Interestingly, on returning home, I looked up the hotel on Trip Advisor (naturally intending to write a stinker of a review). Review after review complained about the same matters as had upset us, plus a lot more serious things that it's better not to relate. The response in every case was one of those standard cut-and-paste responses along the lines of, "We are sorry we fell below our normal standards on this occasion, we will take everything you say on board, blah blah …" In other words, because they have a captive clientèle who need to be near the airport, they couldn't give a shit.

The flight in the morning was an early one, so my Casio watch alarm had to be drafted back into action.

Beep beep beep beep beep beep beep beep… - Happy Days.

The transfer offered us a chance to reflect on the lives of the many Uber drivers we had encountered. In Nashville, Paul and I had been driven by a guy who immediately (and without prompting) told us that he was an ex-crack addict, but that he had turned his life around and was now able to earn a living driving people. This seemed very praiseworthy, so we both launched into supportive comments and compliments. Unfortunately, within moments, he was attributing his new life to having Found The Lord, and started spouting some pro-Christian propaganda, which we found less welcome. By the time he had then moved on to praising the skills and triumphs of Donald Trump, we were luckily approaching our destination and able to escape.

In the meantime, we had met people who drive Uber full time, all of whom seemed perfectly happy with their lives. We had also met some who only drive for a few hours each weekend to make some extra pocket money, and at least two who were actually on their first day. The gentleman who took us to the airport in Nashville on that last morning was probably the most unusual driver we had encountered. The car was particularly neat, clean and tidy and, in what we could only assume was an attempt to get good reviews, he had displayed a small collection of freebies on the back seat. These included water, soft drinks, sweets and other snacks, as well as napkins and souvenir items such as lighters and keyrings. He revealed that he was a full-time nurse, working twelve-hour shifts and also driving lengthy Uber stints in between. When we asked whether this didn't threaten to make him overtired (our unspoken subtext being that it might impair his driving skills, not to mention his nursing abilities), he revealed that he slept an average of three hours a night and had adopted this lifestyle in order to provide well for his family, including his three small children. It seemed churlish to suggest that spending more time with them might actually be a better policy, but he got us to the airport efficiently and the flight home was pretty much the same as the flight over: straightforward and easy.

A book like this ought to have some kind of ending, but the only ending you can really have to a travel book is to finish the journey, which we were able to do by being picked up from Southampton airport by friends, before retiring to bed for twenty-four hours.

Having never been a fan of beach holidays, I was happy to have spent three weeks meeting new people, seeing new places and learning new things. None of it would have been possible without the incredible Birgit. Her tolerance and open-minded keenness to try out new things, and her willingness to put up with my obsessions and quirks, mean that I am truly blessed.

"Shall we do it again next year?"

"Er, no. Next year, I'm due for my beach holiday."

"Fair enough."

Also by Oliver Gray:

VOLUME
A cautionary tale of rock and roll obsession

V.A.C.A.T.I.O.N.
Cautionary tales of travelling without style

ALAB (with Eddie Hardin)
35 years of musical mayhem on the road with the Spencer Davis Group

ACCESS ONE STEP
The official history of the Joiner's Arms

ZANDER
An Americana whodunnit

All published by Sarsen Press, Winchester, UK